THE FURTHER LETTERS OF

HENRY ROOT

H ROOT ESQ.
139 ELM PARK MANS
PARK WALK.
LONDON SW

H. Root Esq.,
139 Elm Park Mansic
Park Walk,
London, SW10.

Lord Root,
Chairman & Chief Exective
Henry Root Wet Fish,
139 Elm Park Mansions,
Park Walk,
LONDON S.W.10.

InternationalManagementGroup
58 Queen Anne Street · London W1M 0DX · England · 01-486 7171
London · Cleveland · Johannesburg · Los Angeles · New York · Tokyo · Paris · Christ

ROYAL COLLEGE OF SURGEONS OF ENGLAND
LONDON WC2A 3PN

H Root Es
139 Elm Pa
Park Wal

FOREIGN AND
POST
-7 JUN 1979
COMMONWEALTH OFFIC

BBC

H. Root, Esq.,
139 Elm Park Mansic
Park Walk,
LONDON,
SW10.

Mr H Root
139 Elm Park Mansions
Park Walk
London S.W.10

Lord Root
139 Elm Park Mansions
Park Walk,
S.W.10

H. Root E
139 Elm P
Park We
SW 10

OFFICE

8 NOV
1979

H. Root, Esq.,
139 Elm Park Mansions,
Park Walk, S.W.10.
London, S.W.10.

H. Root Esq.
139 Elm Park M
Park Walk
London SW

HOUSE OF COMMONS

Henry Root
139 Elm Pa
Park Walk,
London S.W.10.

Ted Heath

THE FURTHER LETTERS OF
HENRY ROOT

WEIDENFELD AND NICOLSON
LONDON

Design concept devised by Behram Kapadia
Letters photographed by Geoff Goode

ISBN 0 297 77853 6

Printed in Great Britain by Butler & Tanner Ltd,
Frome and London

For the future Mrs Root,
Doreen and Henry Jr.

139 Elm Park Mansions
Park Walk
London, S.W.10.

Mrs Thatcher,
10 Downing Street,
London, S.W.1.   24th July 1979.

Dear Prime Minister,

<u>Double</u> the VAT on theatre tickets, that's my advice!

Strolling down Whitehall this afternoon on business that needn't concern you, I ran head-first into a rabble of chanting rowdies, many of whom were in full make-up even though it was not yet tea-time. Taking it to be a student demo out of hand, I cried "slash student grants!" and passed among them with my stick. It was then that one old party, whom I took to be a teacher, announced that they were in fact actors marching to No 10 in protest against the price of theatre seats.

On hearing this, I naturally redoubled my efforts, realising that you wouldn't want the decision-making processes to be interrupted by a march of painted mimes. I tried to head them back to their various play-houses and rehearsal-rooms, but many got through, I fear, and for this I blame myself.

Don't misunderstand me, Prime Minister. This is a free country for those who can afford it and I would always defend the right of jugglers and ballet dancers to pursue their activities in authorised places. What I <u>do</u> object to, however, is that their efforts to amuse should be subsidised out of the pockets of tax-payers.

It so happens that my own play THE ENGLISH WAY OF DOING THINGS by HENRY ROOT will shortly be opening at the Vaudeville Theatre in the Strand. Should it fail to attract an audience, I won't run bleating to Norman St John Stevas, the boulevardier, demanding that he support it out of public funds.

There are many theatres in the West End occupying prime sites for the purveyance of hamburgers and soda. Such as cannot pay their way should be pulled down and reconstituted on a sound commercial footing.

Cut back subsidies to the arts!

Your man on the door-step,

Henry Root

Henry Root.

Chancellor of the Duchy of Lancaster

Henry Root Esq
139 Elm Park Mansions
Park Walk
LONDON SW10

Dear Mr Root,

Your letter of 24th July which you sent to
the Prime Minister about the Equity demon-
stration has been passed to the Chancellor
of the Duchy of Lancaster who is responsible
for the Arts.

The Chancellor is at present abroad on an
official visit but I am sure that he would
be most interested to read your views and
I will bring your letter to his attention
on his return.

Yours sincerely

Miss M G E Giles
Private Secretary

139 Elm Park Mansions
Park Walk
London, S.W.10.

The Picture Editor,
The Daily Express,   1st May 1979.
Fleet Street,
London, E.C.4.

Dear Sir,
          Enclosed you will find a selection of prints typical of my
work. They are entitled:

          Ducks on Pond.

          Old Greek Saddler and Wife.

          Nude with Banana.

          My Cat Ben.

          Footpath with Sign Post.

          A Beach Somewhere.

          I am slowly building up a photo library (approx 400 new pics
per year) of the urban and rural environment. I use a Hasselblad
616X for maximum sharpness and expense.

          I am prepared to accept commissioned work exclusively on a
free-lance basis.

          I enclose a stamped addressed envelope in case you are unable
to utilise any of these prints at the moment.

          Yours faithfully,

          Henry de Root

          Henry de Root. Photographer.

DAILY EXPRESS   Express
                      Newspapers
                      Limited

                      121 Fleet Street
                      London EC4P 4JT
                      Telephone
                      01-353 8000
                      Telex No 21841
                      Cable Address
                      Express London

9th May, 1979

Henry de Root,
139 Elm Park Mansions,
Park Walk,
London, S.W.10

Dear Mr. de Root,

Thank you very much for sending the photographs,
but I am afraid they are not suitable for
publication in the Daily Express.

Enclosed are the photographs.

yours sincerely,

Andrew Harvey
<u>Picture Editor</u>

enc.

Registered in London No 141748.
Registered office: 121 Fleet St London EC4P 4JT

139 Elm Park Mansions
Park Walk
London, S.W.10.

The Resident Team,
'Junior That's Life',
The BBC,
London, W.12.   11th August 1979.

Dear Team,

I gather that you want to make monkeys of singing grannies on 'Junior That's Life'.

What a great idea!

I'd like to nominate Mrs Root's mother, Enid Potts, aged 79. She's no Shirley Bassey, but she is bad. Her repertoire consists mainly of excerpts from 'The Dancing Years', but she occasionally essays some of the up-to-date stuff too. Some years ago she won third prize for her Petunia Clark impression on a senior citizens' away day.

What if the old tart kicks the bucket on camera? It would be good TV, but what about recompense? Will you have her insured?

I suppose that as with senior 'That's Life' you are presently looking for healthily vulgar contributions from the general public. I append hereunder a new ode which I hope you will consider apposite in the circumstances.

        'There was an old granny from Chislehurst
        Who before she could pee had to whistle first.
        One sad day in June
        She quite lost the tune
        And what do you know? - her bladder!!'

Not bad, eh? Will Cyril be with you to read out these contributions from the viewing public? I think it might be more amusing to have a knowing little basket aged eight in Cyril's chair. Still, not for me to advise. You know what you're doing. When would you like me to wheel Mrs Root's mother in for an audition?

Cheers!

Henry Root.

Henry Root.

M
```
   889077 PO FD G
   299992 PO TS G
```

H71 1133 LONDON TELEX 26

HENRY ROOT 139 ELMPARK MANSIONS PARK WALK
LONDONSW10

PLEASE RING BBC THATS LIFE RE SINGING GRANNY REVERSING CHARGES
01 743 1272 EXTENSION 6374/5
   REGARDS CHRIS SERLE

COL 139 SW10 C1 743 1272 6374/5
   299992 PO TS G
   889077 PO FD G

139 Elm Park Mansions
Park Walk
London, S.W.10.

The Earl of Longford,
Sidgwick and Jackson Ltd,
1 Tavistock Chambers,
London, W.C.1.   11th August 1979.

Dear Lord Longford,

 I read recently that Miss Mary Kenny is doing you a book on
God. That's one to look forward to! Well done! Will it be in the
shops in time for Christmas! That's always a good idea. Catch
the mugs with money in their pockets and long shopping-lists. Pro-
moted with verve I can see this one being as big a stocking-filler
as Ronnie Barker's 'Book of Bedtime Boobs'.

 Miss Kenny's concept has given me this solid idea. Why not
a series of similar books? That is to say, studies by ordinary
unqualified folk like Miss Kenny of great thinkers and their influence. Such a series, unlike the stuff written by University boffins,
would be readily intelligible to the man in the street.

 I was talking over the idea with my daughter Doreen (20), who
is reading philosophy and sociology at Essex University and who
therefore thinks she knows more about these things than I do, and
in no time at all she had come up with the enclosed outline for
such a series.

 I hope you like it. If you do, I suggest you appoint my
Doreen as General Editor. She'll be leaving Essex in a year and I'm
sure she'd be happy to work with you.

 I enclose a stamped addressed envelope for the safe return
of my Doreen's outline, should you not wish to utilise the concept
at this time. I should warn you, perhaps, that the idea is fully
protected by The Copyright Act (1957), so I don't advise you to
'borrow' it to your advantage without due credit to myself! I know
what you publsihers are like!

 Let's make money on this one!

 Yours sincerely,

Henry Root

Henry Root.

Enc: Draft outline for SEMINAL THINKERS IN A NUTSHELL - a new series
  edited by DOREEN ROOT.

SEMINAL THINKERS IN A NUTSHELL.
General Editor - DOREEN ROOT.

Draft Series.

God - Mary Kenny.
Plato - Jimmy Hill.
Christ - Miss Vicki Hodge.
Hegel - Richard Afton.
Marx - Arthur Askey.
Tolstoy - Richard Ingrams.
Nietzsche - Diana Dors.
Darwin - Christopher Booker.
Popper - Malcolm Allison (Big Mal!)
Sir Winston Churchill - Dr Patrick Cosgrave (Mrs Thatcher's chirop-
                                                                odist).
Lenin - Carol Channing.
Mohammed Ali - Taki (the little Jap).
Aristotle - Shirley Conran (the cook).
Newton - James Herriot (the vet).
Freud - Anna Raeburn.
Chomsky - Richard West.
Kant - Jean Rook.
Descartes - Patricia Boxall.
Einstein - Michael Parkinson.
Mrs Thatcher - George Gale.

SIDGWICK & JACKSON
Limited
PUBLISHERS

Telegrams: Watergate, London
Telephones: 01-242 6081/2 3

Place of Registration: London, England
Registered Number of Company: 100126

Registered Office:

1 Tavistock Chambers

Bloomsbury Way, London W.C.1A 2SG

20th September 1979

Dear Mr. Root

Thank you for your letter of September 15th.   I have now had an opportunity of studying your earlier letter and the very interesting proposals put forward by your daughter. Please allow me respectfully to congratulate you on some excellent ideas.

Alas! we ourselves would not be able to make use of them, but I do hope that you would find a more enterprising publisher.

May I apologise if I have been a long time in replying to you, due to myself and my secretary being on holiday for the last month.

Yours sincerely
with no mean apologies
Frank
Taylor

Henry Root, Esq
139 Elm Park Mansions
Park Walk
S.W.10

139 **Elm Park Mansions**
Park Walk
London, S.W.10.

Mr Michael Wolff,
Wolff Olins Ltd,
22 Dukes Road,
London, W.C.1.   14th August 1979.

Dear Mr Wolff,

I recently saw your firm featured in 'About Business' on
Thames TV and I was quite impressed. By <u>you</u>, that is. Your
partner, Olins, made a frightful nonsense, if you remember, of
creating a new 'image' for a kraut Count whose pencil company
had gone back badly. His brief was to come up with a new design
scheme which emphasised all the products the company made <u>other</u>
than pencils. Olins and his men went into a creative trance
which lasted for some weeks and then flew, with evidence of
their labours, back to Germany. The board were called to a
meeting at which Olins ran his new visual image up the flag-pole.
And what was it? A pencil! It wasn't until you were called
in that a 'concept' was thrashed out which met with the Cunt's
approval. Well done!

Do you create 'images' for the man in the street, or do
you deal only in company 'images'?

I ask because I'm currently going flat out for a seat in
the Lords under Mrs Thatcher and when I become Lord Root I want
to measure up. As it happens, I'm not too concerned about myself,
but Mrs Root causes misgivings. I enclose some photos of ourselves
taken at a recent outing and as you can see she's not too sweet.
Can you do anything with her? If not, I may have to dump her.
I imagine I wouldn't be the first life peer compelled to take
this step. Where, after all, is <u>Lord</u> Falkender on state occasions
which involve Black Rod and others? Conspicuous by his absence!

I must emphasise that I want this account to be handled by
you personally, and not by Olins. I can't afford to be messed
about the way the kraut Count was.

Let me have your prices on a top-to-toe 'image' job.

Yours sincerely,

Henry Root

Henry Root.

Mr Henry Root
139 Elm Park Mansions
Park Walk
London SW10

30 August 1979

Dear Mr Root

I am just back from a swimming holiday in France
and have just seen your most intriguing letter.

The problem you pose is a familiar one. We often
have requests of this kind. It is difficult to say
whether anything substantial can be done or not
merely by looking at the photographs, and I
recommend that before Wolff Olins makes any formal
proposal to you, we carry out the following
procedure which will give me a better idea of what
is possible in your particular case.

At a mutually convenient time, I suggest that both
Mrs Root and you walk from Victoria Station through
Green Park to the Ritz Hotel where you have afternoon tea. In addition to this, and on another
occasion, I suggest that you have dinner with
Mrs Root in the Connaught Hotel. I will make arrangements for someone from Wolff Olins to be there to
observe, either myself or one of our senior consul-
tants but certainly not Wally Olins. From this we
would get an idea of how you behave together, both
in a relaxed situation and formally in public. This
would give us a much better basis on which to see
how we could contribute and what sort of fees you
should expect to pay. We would not charge you any
fees for this preliminary investigation, but we
would expect you to cover our expenses.

2

Thank you so much for your enquiry. I am glad
you enjoyed the TV programme.

Yours sincerely

Michael Wolff

PS
It would be sensible not to inform
Mrs Root at this stage.

139 Elm Park Mansions
Park Walk
London, S.W.10.

Mr Michael Wolff,
Wolff Olins Ltd,
22 Dukes Road,
London, W.C.1.

6th September 1979.

Dear Mr Wolff,

Thank you for your letter of 30th August.

You seem to have grasped the concept well and your suggestion that you should monitor me and Mrs Root in an observation situation meets with my approval.

Due to Mrs Root's leg, however, it would not be advisable to undertake the slow walk from Victoria to the Ritz Hotel. I suggest we commence the manoeuvre at the Ritz and accordingly Mrs Root and I will take tea in the foyer there between 4 and 5 pm on Monday 24th September. Should there be dancing to a trio you will find our performance adequate if lacking in elaboration.

Mrs Root would be suspicious were I to escort her in public twice in the same calender month, so I suggest that 'Operation Connaught Hotel' should take place on the evening of Friday 5th October. If you would care to let me know that this date is con-venient for you, I will make the necessary booking.

I take it you will bill me in thses two matters when you deliver your initial report and comments.

No doubt you will wish to hang on to the photographs of myself and Mrs Root for identification purposes, but I must ask you to keep them in a safe place. It would be difficult to explain their permanent loss to Mrs Root who keeps and album.

I look forward to doing business with you image-wise.

Yours sincerely,

Henry Root

Henry Root.

Mr Henry Root
139 Elm Park Mansions
Park Walk
London SW10

13 September 1979

Dear Mr Root

Thank you for your letter. Friday 5th October is
fine but I'm afraid Monday 24th September is not
suitable. I could manage the 26th, 27th or 28th,
and I would be grateful if you could let me know
which of these is convenient for both of you as
soon as possible.

Please be assured that your photographs are absolutely safe.

Yours sincerely

Michael Wolff

---

139 Elm Park Mansions
Park Walk
London, S.W.10.

Mr Michael Wolff,
Wolff Olins Ltd,
22 Dukes Road,
London, W.C.1.

19th September 1979.

Dear Mr Wolff,

Thank you for your letter of 13th September, which (due, no
doubt, to the extraordinary performance of Sir William Barlow) has
only just arrived on my desk.

You seem to be on the ball. Well done. I like that in a
man.

Of the dates you suggest for 'Operation Tea at the Ritz',
the 28th of this month would be the most suitable. If I hear
nothing further from you, Mrs Root and I will be observable from
a position in the foyer between 4 and 5 pm on that day.

Perhaps it would be best if you were to submit both reports
after stage 2 - 'Operation Dinner at the Connaught' on Friday 5th
October. Do you wish me to effect a booking for you on the 5th,
or can you arrange that yourself? And for how many will it be?
I would expect your operative to have an observational assistant,
but I wouldn't like to suppose he'd take advantage of the situation
to give his 'personal secretary' a night on the tiles. I shall be
vetting his expenses most carefully.

Yours sincerely,

Henry Root

Henry Root.

WOLFF OLINS

Mr Henry Root
139 Elm Park Mansions
Park Walk
London SW10

2 October 1979

Dear Mr Root

Since you were not able to be at the Ritz
or able to let me know that you weren't
going to be there, I suppose that you probably either wish to postpone or not to
proceed with the project, so unless I hear
from you before Friday, we will not be at
the Connaught.

Yours sincerely

Michael Wolff

---

139 Elm Park Mansions
Park Walk
London, S.W.10.

Mr Michael Wolff,
Wolff Olins Ltd,
22 Dukes Road,
London, W.C.1.

3rd October 1979.

Dear Mr Wolff,

What on earth's going on? Mrs Root and I were in position
at the appointed time and partook of tea and sandwiches for the
specified period.

I assumed that the couple in hats lurking two tables away
were yourself and a female operative. Small wonder that my various
signals unsettled them to the point of departure early.

If you failed for some reason to attend I will have to pass
my expenses in the matter over to you. Unless, that is, you redeem
yourself somewhat by performing better in the course of Stage 2 -
'Operation Dinner at the Connaught Hotel' this Friday. Mrs Root
and I will certainly be there participating a la carte and I trust
you will be present too.

For goodness sake let's not have another cock-up!

Yours sincerely,

Henry Root.

139 Elm Park Mansions
Park Walk
London, S.W.10.

Mr Geoffrey Wheatcroft,
The Spectator,
56 Doughty Street,   23rd August 1979.
London, W.C.1.

Dear Mr Wheatcroft,

     I gather you are the Literary Editor of 'The Spectator'. The style has greatly improved of late and I take it you are responsible for this. Well done! All the contributors now commence each paragraph with some such urbane remark as 'Trollope would have been amused by....', 'Wasn't it Flaubert who said....', 'After an agreeable lunch with....' etc etc. This is excellent and most civilised.

     I have recently commissioned myself to put together an anthology of great modern British prose, to show that proud and stately phrase-making didn't die with Dornford Yates, and I wonder whether I might have your permission to quote the following passages which have appeared in your journal.

1. Dr Patrick Cosgrave writing about the late Airey Neave:

    'On the last occasion I saw Airey, he said: "I know one thing. When they come for me it will be from behind. They aren't soldier enough to look me in the face".

2. Mr Richard West in 'The Spectator' of 16th June 1979.

    'I was sad to read of the death in Zimbabwe of Major André Dennison, who only recently won the country's top award for courage.. He was a witty and most agreeable drinking companion. I notice he received his last, fatal bullet resisting a ZANLA attack on the ~~the~~ bar of the Zimbabwe Ruins Hotel. He would have liked to have gone that way.'

3. Mr Taki in 'The Spectator' of 4th August 1979.

    'The last two years of his life he suffered terribly. Both of his legs were amputated. Needless to say he never complained. He died without tears. Although I am a Christian there are times when I begin to doubt. Why should Tony Galento have suffered?'

4. Mr George Gale in 'The Spectator' of 18th August 1979.

    'If the captain of a ship left the deck knowing a storm was imminent he would lose his command. If a foreign correspondent left his base, knowing big stories were about to break, he would lose his posting. Mr Atkins is a former naval officer. He knows about discipline and he knows about duty. As Northern Ireland Secretary he possesses proconsular and vice-regal powers: under direct rule he is Northern Ireland's ruler. He must have known that August was ominous'.

    I look forward to receiving the necessary permissions to quote these fine and ringing passages.

    Yours sincerely,

Henry Root

    Henry Root.

Spectator

56 Doughty Street London WC1N 2LL Telephone 01-405 1706 Telegrams Spectator London Telex 27124

Henry Root Esq.,
139 Elm Park Mansions,
London SW10

20 September 1979

Dear Mr Root,

I am sorry that you had no reply to your letter of 23 August. Unfortunately Geoffrey Wheatcroft is on holiday at the moment and will not therefore be able to answer your enquiry about reprinting the Hope-Wallace obituary until his return at the beginning of next month. Though the party conferences will be taking much of his time just then I will try to ensure that you get an answer as soon as possible.

I am so sorry about the delay.

Yours sincerely,

Clare Asquith

Clare Asquith

Mr Richard Ryder,
10 Downing Street,
London, S.W.1.

139 Elm Park Mansions
Park Walk
London, S.W.10.

30th August 1979.

Dear Ryder,

The Prime Minister's courageous Ulster initiative last week was an inspiration to ordinary folk throughout the land! Please tell her this from me.

Never has she seemed less like a woman and more like a Tory! The shots of her on TV and her cry of "Let me speak to my people!" as she broke away from her security guards and reached out both hands to the cheering common folk made one proud to be English for the first time since we dumped the Hun at Wembley in '66.

Is it possible to obtain a photograph of her in battle-dress and combat helmet snapped at the precise moment, as shown on TV, when the wind from her personal helicopter blew up her skirt to reveal World War 2 Women's Airforce knickers worn below the knee? How her enemies must have trembled!

I enclose a pound to cover the expense.

Incidentally, I have recently been in contact with old Major Wyldbore-Smith at Conservative HQ about the possibility of an honour for myself in the Prime Minister's new year list. I pointed out that I was prepared to make a substantial contribution to party funds, but he has indicated that titles can't be purchased from the Tories!

Could you tell the old duffer to smarten up? You'll appreciate how I'd hate to join the Liberals!

Yours sincerely,

Henry Root

Henry Root.

Let's have further initiatives here and there!

10 DOWNING STREET

7th September 1979

Dear Mr Root,

I am writing to thank you very much indeed for
your letter of 30th August.

In answer to your request for a photograph
of the Prime Minister, taken while she was in
Ulster, I am afraid that we do not have the
photograph and I would suggest that you write
direct to the newspaper concerned. I am
returning the pound which you enclosed.

With best wishes,

Yours sincerely,

Richard Ryder
Political Office

Henry Root Esq

139 Elm Park Mansions
Park Walk
London, S.W.10.

The Editor,
Burke's Peerage,
56 Walton Street,
London, S.W.3.

4th September 1979.

Dear Sir,

I would appreciate your advice on a certain matter.

Having supported the Tories steadily for some time now I expect to be raised to the peerage in the near future.

I naturally wish to have my new cutlery, matching shot-guns, luggage and stationary (duly embossed and crested) ready in good time for answering communications from others in respect of weekends in the country shooting this and that, so I am giving some thought to what my title should be.

I would prefer, of course, to be Lord Root, but I have a suspicion that there was once a car dealer of this name, and for all I know there still might be. I certainly wouldn't want to be confused with him, particularly since I recall his wife rather letting him down in public by wearing leopard-skin drawers and standing on her head. Or was that Lady Docker? Anyway, what happens in this sort of double-up situation? Could he be per-suaded to change his name? Perhaps to Lord Warren Street? I am not without means.

Are you experts too on forebears and heraldic matters? I have in mind my coat of arms and am considering (since I have spent my life in fish) two prawns rampant and a cock crab en suivant.

I'd appreciate your advice at your earliest convenience.

Yours faithfully,

Henry Root

Henry Root.

Burke's Peerage Limited

PUBLISHERS

56 Walton Street London SW3 1RB   Telephone 01-584 8134 and 1106
Registered No. 210290 England   Registered Office: 42 Curzon Street London W1

Henry Root Esq
139 Elm Park Mansions
Park Walk
LONDON
SW10

Wednesday
5 September
1979

Dear Mr Root

Thank you for your letter of 4th September in which
you inquire about whether the can be two Lord Roots.

To the best of our knowledge there is no Lord Root.
There is however, a Lord Rootes which could be the
Peer you were thinking of.

I hope this information has been of some value to you.

Yours sincerely

P.P. Katherine Heneage

Felicity Mortimer

Chairman & Managing Director Jeremy Norman. *Directors* John Brooke-Little MVO (Richmond Herald of Arms).
John Cook. The Earl of Lichfield. Dr. Remington Norman. Hugo Vickers. Felicity Mortimer.

139 Elm Park Mansions
Park Walk
London, S.W.10.

Mr Bernard Levin,
The Sunday Times,
200 Grays Inn Road,
London, W.C.1.

1st September 1979.

Dear Mr Levin,

You will be interested to hear that Mr Peter Saunders (The
Mousetrap Man!) will shortly be presenting on the West End stage
my original comedy in two acts, THE ENGLISH WAY OF DOING THINGS
by HENRY ROOT. It concerns a Police Commissioner who sets forth
in fair shape to apprehend the inmates of a bawdy-house, but who
is so over-whelmed to discover that they outrank him socially that,
in a side-splitting climax, he finds himself taking the bookings!

On the assumption that 'The Sunday Times' will be back on
the streets in time for the first night, I now enclose a fiver for
yourself to ensure that you review it favourably.

While I have your attention perhaps I could trouble you for
the address of your 'young lady', Miss Arianna Stassinopulos. I'm
eager that Mrs Root should join her Levitation and Deep Personal
Awareness Group as soon as possible. I'm told that city gents
who've joined now wear foam rubber under their bowler hats so that
when in a trance they levitate too sharply to the ceiling they
don't drive their heads on impact clean into their chests. No, I'm
only chaffing, Bernard! As it happens, I don't have much time for
any of this mystical nonsense from the east, with elderly Indians
in their underwear manifesting themselves up ropes, but I dare say
your young lady knows what she's doing and I'm keen to get Mrs
Root out of the house from time to time. If that costs me a hundred
and fifty notes, well it's cheap at the price.

I look forward to hearing from you.

Yours sincerely,

Henry Root

Henry Root.

THE TIMES

Times Newspapers Limited, P.O. Box no. 7, New Printing House Square,
Gray's Inn Road, London WC1X 8EZ (registered office)
Telephone 01-837 1234 Telex 264971 Registered no. 894646 England

6th September 1979

Mr. Bernard Levin regrets he
cannot do as you ask.

139 Elm Park Mansions
Park Walk
London, S.W.10.

R. Alistair McAlpine Esq,
Conservative Board of Finance,
32 Smith Square,
London, S.W.1.   4th September 1979.

Dear McAlpine,

Seeing myself as apt material for a peerage, I wrote to
your Board on 7th August asking how much I would have to slip the
Tories' way to secure a seat in the Lords.

To my surprise, this reasonable question was fielded by
Major-General Wyldbore-Smith and fired back at me stump-high.

"It's not possible to buy a peerage from the Tory Party,"
he said.

Delightful! Well, he's a military man, of course (and nothing
wrong with that) and I expect he's still got his nose so deep into
Queen's Regualtions that he hasn't got time to be as _au courant_ as
you and I with the ways of the world.

I realise now that I should have 'dealt with' you in the
first place. Horses for courses.

I contributed generously to the Tory Party during the recent
election campaign, but I'm realistic enough to understand that I'll
have to do rather better than this to get a peerage.

What would do the trick? £50,000? £100,000?

Perhaps we could meet to discuss the matter? Are you a member
of the Carlton? I'm not, but if we met there, you could enrol me at
the same time. Two birds with one stone. Just give me a date and
time. Perhaps you could make the booking.

Needless to say there would be 'something in this' for you
personally, and I now enclose a pound (for yourself) to show that
I am a serious person.

I look forward to hearing from you.

Support Mrs Thatcher!

Yours sincerely,

Henry Root

Henry Root.

TELEPHONE:
01-222 9000

TELEGRAMS:
CONSTITUTE LONDON SW1

CONSERVATIVE AND UNIONIST CENTRAL OFFICE
TREASURERS' DEPARTMENT.

HONORARY TREASURER
CONSERVATIVE & UNIONIST PARTY
R. ALISTAIR McALPINE
DEPUTY TREASURER
ROBIN HOLLAND-MARTIN

32 SMITH SQUARE
WESTMINSTER, SW1P 3HH

6th September, 1979

<u>PERSONAL</u>

Dear Mr Root

    I am writing to acknowledge receipt of your letter
of the 4th September enclosing a £1 note.

    I am sure you are well aware, and have also been
so informed by General Wyldbore-Smith that there is
absolutely no question of purchasing a peerage from
the Conservative Party. I cannot emphasise this too
strongly.

    No useful purpose can be served by continuing
this correspondence, and I return your £1 note herewith.

        Yours sincerely,

R. ALISTAIR MCALPINE

Henry Root, Esq.,
139 Elm Park Mansions,
Park Walk,
London S.W.10

139 Elm Park Mansions
Park Walk
London, S.W.10.

Mr R. Alistair McAlpine,
Conservative Central Office,
32 Smith Square,
London, S.W.1.   8th September 1979.

Dear McAlpine,

      I am in receipt of your astonishing communication of 6th
September.

      This is to inform you that I have now joined the Liberal
Party.

      Support John Pardoe!

      Yours sincerely,

Henry Root

      Henry Root.

Copy to the Prime Minister.

139 Elm Park Mansions
Park Walk
London, S.W.10.

The Treasurer,
The Liberal Party,
1 Whitehall Place,
London, S.W.1.

11th September 1979.

Sir,
　　Here's a pound! Let's go!
　　Support John Pardoe!
　　Yours faithfully,

Henry Root

Henry Root.

139 Elm Park Mansions
Park Walk
London, S.W.10.

The Treasurer,
The Liberal Party,
1 Whitehall Place,
London, S.W.1.

2nd October 1979.

Sir,

On 11th September I sent you £1, with the promise implied
that there were larger sums in the offing and that I might be on
the point of joining the party.

I haven't heard a word from you!

This is _not_ a very promising start!

I would hate to think that I was about to receive the same
treatment from you as that handed out to my friend Mr 'Union Jack'
Haywood.

Support John Pardoe!

Yours faithfully,

Henry Root

Henry Root.

Telephone: 01-839 4092

LIBERAL PARTY ORGANISATION
HEADQUARTERS

1, Whitehall Place,
London SW1A 2HE.

Henry Root Esq.,
139, Elm Park Mansions,
London, S.W.10.

3rd October 1979

Dear Mr. Root,

Thank you for your kind donation which is
very much appreciated and I apologise for the
delay in sending this acknowledgement.

If you do decide to join the Party please
contact

Miss Edna McGregor (Hon Sec. Chelsea LA)
Flat K8, Sloane Ave. Mansions, SW3.
tel: 584 7754

I am sure they would welcome your support!

In the meantime I enclose a Bankers Order-
should you wish to donate to the Party on a
regular basis

Yours sincerely

Dee Doocey,
Finance Officer

139 Elm Park Mansions
Park Walk
London, S.W.10.

The Rt Hon David Steel,
The House of Commons,   6th October 1979.
Westminster,
London, S.W.1.

Dear Mr Steel,
         No doubt you have on your desk various letters between myself
and your Finance Officer, Mr Dee Doocey, re my joining the Liberals
and contributing towards the pending fund.
         Being new to liberalism I'm afraid I stepped off the pavement
with the wrong foot, as it were, by not checking first as to the
current leadership situation and by closing my letters with 'Support
John Pardoe!' At least I knew it wasn't Jeremy Thorpe! (What was
all the fuss about? I thought Norman St John Scott, so-called 'Gino'
Newton and Peter Bessel got a fair trial. What did you think?).
         Congratulations on your conference showing down in Broadstairs!
I wasn't able to get down there myself to support your motions since
I was flat to the boards last week organising a 'Support the Springbok
Rugby Players' march.
         Might I say that contrary to rumours circulating in the corri-
dors of power I am not the mysterious Mr X referred to recently by Mr
Sam Silkin and pardoned by same as per the old-boy network? I am not
of the old-boy network, nor am I a sodomite. Does this matter? Let
me know.
         Support the SPG! Let's go!
         Yours sincerely,

         Henry Root

         Henry Root. Liberal!

HOUSE OF COMMONS
LONDON SW1A OAA

October 8th 1979.

Dear Mr. Root,

In Mr. Steel's absence abroad I am writing to thank you for
your letter of October 6th and for your generous donation
to Party Funds which we have now sent on to Liberal Party
Headquarters.

Mr. Steel will see this for information on his return to
London and I am sure that he will be most interested to
have your views and most grateful to you for your generosity.

Thank you for taking the trouble to write.

Yours sincerely,

Nali Dislan

Private Office.

Henry Root, Esq.,
139 Elm Park Mansions,
Park Walk,
London S.W.10.

139 Elm Park Mansions
Park Walk
London, S.W.10.

Mrs Shirley Conran,
c/o Sidgwick & Jackson Ltd,
1 Tavistock Chambers,
London, W.C.1.

5th September 1979.

Dear Mrs Conran,

I want you to know that until I read your book 'Superwoman' recently (better late than never!) I had always supposed that a married man had to forego the comforts of a well-run home. Like most men, indeed, I had always assumed that the only way of getting a decent meal on time was to cook it oneself or hire a chef. You have done much, it seems to me, to remove this silly prejudice against female house-keepers and have, by and large, put women back in the kitchen where they belong. Even Mrs Root can now boil an egg as well as any man. Well done!

Not that you recommend a life of unremitting drudgery for the ladies! Far from it! You seem to believe in plenty of relaxation too, as we discover on page 48 of your book, where you announce, with more pride than discretion, perhaps:

'I've just given one to each of the men in my life. They seemed pathetically grateful. I felt almost guilty!'

<u>Good</u> for you, Shirley, I thought, but why feel guilty? Even we senior citizens have to uncorset ourselves from time to time. When I reached the end of the book, however, I did begin to feel that perhaps you had been spreading yourself rather more thinly than a lady mindful of her reputation ought. Here, under the provocative heading 'How to get hold of the men in your life!', you tell us who these favoured fellows are. And a pretty impressive line-up they make! They are, in no particular order, as far as I can tell: your doctor, dentist, insurance broker, taxi driver, bank manager (very sensible!), milkman, vet, decorator, plumber, carpenter, electrician, TV repair man, newspaper boy, florist and various unspecified functionaries at the local police station, station, hospital and town hall.

Wow! Superwoman indeed!

Could you oblige with a photo, Shirley? I believe you reside in France due to your tax situation (nothing wrong with that) so I am enclosing a pound to cover the costs.

Yours admiringly,

Henry Root.

Henry Root.

Monte Carlo
4 December 1979

Dear Mr Root,

How very kind of you to write to me! I was delighted to get your letter — and how thoughtful of you to enclose a pound note. I shall buy a bottle of wine with it and drink to the health of Mr & Mrs. Root!

With best wishes

Shirley Conran

Shirley Conran, author of SUPERWOMAN.
Crown Publishers, Inc.

139 Elm Park Mansions
Park Walk
London, S.W.10.

Mr Cliff Richard,
'Top of the Pops!'
BBC TV,   5th September 1979.
London, W.12.

Dear Cliff,

        You won't mind my calling you Cliff. We must be about the
same age, you and I. You're a credit to the over-forties, Cliff!
Twenty years at the top and still No 1!

        Con-grat-u-laaaaations!

        So they call you the pop of the tops, the father of them all!
That's absurd You never fathered anyone - unlike some. Nor did
you ever do anything unexpected with a chocolate bar (see Tom
Davies's veiled reference in last week's 'Observer' to this practice
vis-à-vis Miss Marianne Faithful.)

        Could you oblige with a photo, Cliff? You're Mrs Root's
favourite crooner. When I mentioned your name to my boy Henry Jr
(15) he observed that you are now working behind the cosmetics
counter in the Chingford branch of Boots the chemist, but it
transpired that he was confusing you with Miss Yana, the blonde
chanteuse of the early '50s. Remember her, Cliff?

        Cheers!

        Henry Root
        Henry Root.

139 Elm Park Mansions
Park Walk
London, S.W.10.

The Rt Reverend Robert Runcie MC,
The Bishop's Palace,
St Albans,
Herts.

9th September 1979.

Your Grace,

So - you made it all the way to the top spot! Well done!
Here's a pound. It's my experience that you chaps with your collars
back to front seldom say no to a little something for the collection.
Nothing wrong with that. You don't do much harm, in my opinion, so
good luck to you!

From what I've read in the papers you sound suitable material
for Canterbury. According to 'The Observer' you are a witty, polished
man who keeps pigs, had a good war, admires P.G. Wodehouse, supports
Luton Town, plays tennis and squash, was once on the wine committee
of the Athenaeum and knows his way around the world. Well done!
Just what's needed in these confusing times!

I read in 'The Evening Standard' that your better half, Mrs
Runcie, can't bear a lot of religious carry-on. "To me it's not
what I believe in," she said. "Too much religion makes me go off
pop". Surely she doesn't include Cliff Richard in this? His work
has always struck me as compatible with God's mysterious ways.
Otherwise I agree with her. Like her, I'm not a conventionally
religious man. I don't go to church or anything like that, but
if I was involved in an accident I think I'd say my prayers. My
daughter Doreen, who's studying philosophy at Essex University (for
all the good it's doing her) says that this is merely a modern
version of Pascal's best bet argument. What's she talking about?
Have you any idea?

I was particularly pleased to read the editorial in 'The Sunday
Telegraph' which said: 'Dr Runcie has never, unlike some other
prelates, seen the role of the priest in terms of a superior wel-
fare officer; never doubted that God's kingdom is not of this world'.
Hear! Hear! My position precisely! I've worked hard for my pile
and I don't want some do-gooder in the pulpit telling me that I
should redistribute it among the weak and lazy. Let's go on gulling
the unfortunate into expecting their share in the hereafter!

Many deep thinkers such as Malcolm Muggeridge, Mary Kenny,
Christopher Booker and Richard West have been much influenced in
arriving at this point of view by the Reith Lectures of a Dr Edward
Norman with their emphasis on the essentially <u>spiritual</u> nature of
Our Lord's message. Did you hear them? My daughter Doreen says
that by putting the hocus-pocus back into Christianity and evacu-
ating it of all ethical content, Dr Norman has performed the useful
function of making religion unintelligible even to sympathetic
humanists - but what can you expect from a slip of a girl reading
philosophy at a red-brick university?

Let's keep ethics out of religion, religion out of politics
and politics out of sport!

Up the Springboks!

Support Mrs Thatcher! (She put you where you are today!)

Yours faithfully,

Henry Root

Henry Root.

The Rt Rev Robert Runcie MC,
The Bishop's Palace,
St Albans,
Herts.

139 Elm Park Mansions
Park Walk
London, S.W.10.

21st October 1979.
Trafalgar Day! Let's go!

Your Grace,

To put it mildly ('Blessed are the meek'!) I am astonished
not to have received any acknowledgement from you of my letter of
9th September, in which I was good enough to enclose a pound for
your roof.

This was not much, I realise, but I would not like to think
that you can only be bothered to thank folk who send you more substantial contributions.

May I remind you that it is easier for a rich man to enter
the Kingdom of God than a camel?

You may be rather busy at the moment, but surely you could
have designated a junior (what's the Dean doing?) to help with the
mail?

At least you've had time to issue an edict confirming that
there is no place in the church for homosexualists. Well done! But let's
reply to our letters too!

This is the kind of muscular Chistianity we need.

Support Mrs Thatcher!

Render unto Caesar etc!

Yours sincerely,

Henry Root

Henry Root.

The Bishop of St Albans
Abbey Gate House, St Albans, Hertfordshire AL3 4HD
ST ALBANS 53305

24th October, 1979.

Dear Mr. Root,

I write immediately to apologise unreservedly for my failure
to reply to your letter of the 9th September.

It is no doubt good for my pride since we think that we have
an excellent answer system and have already dealt with several thousands
and had no complaints; but there is no doubt at all that we slipped up
with your donation and your letter.   It was in a small pile marked
'for further consideration'.   We eliminated that sort of pile after the
first few days but about three letters remained in it.

I still do not quite know what to make of your mixture but you
seem to write with robust good humour so God bless you.

Yours sincerely,

Robert St Albans

Henry Root, Esq.,
139 Elm Park Mansions,
Park Walk,
London, S.W.10.

139 Elm Park Mansions
Park Walk
London, S.W.10.

Mr And Peter Forster,
The Evening Standard,
47 Shoe Lane,
London, E.C.4.   6th September 1979.

Dear Mr And Peter Forster,

     I assume from your name that you come originally from
Sweden, Finland or Norway. Not your fault. Good luck to you.

     You seem to be settling in well and you write agreeably for
a foreigner (if somewhat affectedly - over here we express ourselves
in a rather more masculine prose.)

     I do object most strongly, however, to your suggestion in
yesterday's 'Evening Standard' that we should all carry identity
cards to assist in the easy arrest and deportation of tourists.

     Such invasion of the citizen's right to privacy may be all
right where you come from, but had you lived among us for a little
longer you would know that such practices are contrary to our
hard-won freedoms.

     Writing as you do for a Tory paper, you should know that in
the last war many millions of Tories gave up their lives <u>fighting</u>
such things as the obligatory carriage of identity discs and com-
pulsory finger-printing on the spot.

     I look forward to your correcting this lapse in a future
column.

     Jeres! (as you no doubt say in your country!)

        Henry Root

        Henry Root.

139 Elm Park Mansions
Park Walk
London, S.W.10.

Sir Keith Joseph,
23 Mulberry Walk,
London, S.W.3.

6th September 1979.

Dear Sir Keith,
    I was sorry to read in yesterday's evening papers that your
house was recently burglarised while you were elsewhere propounding
the moral virtues of private enterprise.
    I'm sure you'll be able to see the funny side of it!
    I expect your mistake was to inform the robbery squad at
your local police station that your house would be empty. That's
always asking for trouble (unless, of course, one wants to make a
quick killing on one's over-insured valuables!)
    You'd be the last person, of course, to disapprove of the
police's reasonable habit of diversification after dark into more
profitable lines. Market forces naturally compel them to subsidise
their still meagre pay-packets with a little entrepreneurial activity
on their own account.
    Here's a pound. Not much, but you're a fine man and if Tories
everywhere sent you a pound you'd soon be able to replace what was
burgled.
    I'm rather long in Grand Metropolitan at the moment. Would
you advise me to hang on or get out while I'm ahead? Horse's mouth,
and all that.
    Support Mrs Thatcher!
    Even the police are monetarists now! Let's go!
    Yours sincerely,

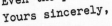

    Henry Root.

DEPARTMENT OF INDUSTRY
ASHDOWN HOUSE
123 VICTORIA STREET
LONDON SW1E 6RB
TELEPHONE DIRECT LINE 01 212 3301
SWITCHBOARD 01 212 7676

Henry Root Esq

12 September 1979

Dear Mr Root,

Thank you for your kind letter and your thoughtful contribution. I am rather puzzled about the £1 - and shall give it to the next deserving flag day.

It was particularly quixotic on your part to send me the £1, since you clearly think that I am the Joseph of Grand Metropolitan. I am not. He is no relation whatsoever - and I am certainly in no position to advise you whether to hang on to those or any other shares. But you and I both believe in the market economy with its choice.

Yours,

Keith Joseph.

139 Elm Park Mansions
Park Walk
London, S.W.10.

Mr Peregrine Worsthorne,
The Sunday Telegraph,
135 Fleet Street,
London, E.C.4.

6th September 1979.

Dear Mr Worsthorne,

My attention has only recently been drawn to an astonishing attack you made some months ago in 'The Sunday Telegraph' on that fine man Lord Longford.

'That Lord Longford should team up with Janie Jones, the convicted procuress', you wrote, 'may not at first glance seem to be a matter meritting much adverse comment. It might even be thought desirable, and a mark of a civilised society, for such a universally execrated wretch to have at least one friend in high places'.

Well! Calling Lord Longford a universally execrated wretch is irresponsible journalism at its worst, in my opinion, and I would strenuously dispute that Miss Janie Jones moves in high places. That she is well-connected I wouldn't deny, but I do not agree that she <u>herself</u> is welcome in the best drawing-rooms, except in her capacity of, as it were, chauffeuse and bunny-mother. It was her custom, when I used to avail myself of her services to supply the 'artistes', at certain local Tory Party functions, to deliver 'the cabaret' at some titled person or cabinet minister's home then leave. I do not recall that she ever hob-nobbed on a social level with those who later, and quite rightly, took it to be their duty to queue up in their pin-stripe suits and Old Etonian ties to give evidence against her.

I await your explanation for this extraordinary outburst.

Yours sincerely,

Henry Root.

Henry Root.

SUNDAY TELEGRAPH

135 FLEET STREET LONDON EC4P 4BL TELEPHONE: 01-353 4242 TELEGRAMS: TELESUN LONDON EC4
TELEX: 22874 TELENEWS LONDON

7th September, 1979

Henry Root, Esq.,
139 Elm Park Mansions,
Park Walk,
London S.W.10

Dear Mr Root,

I am afraid you have rather misread that
article. I never called Lord Longford "a
universally execrated wretch" as will become
clear if you study the piece more carefully.

Yours sincerely,

Peregrine "orsthorne
Associate Editor

SUNDAY TELEGRAPH LIMITED REGISTRATION NO. 667848 ENGLAND
REGISTERED OFFICE 135 FLEET STREET LONDON EC4P 4BL

139 Elm Park Mansions
Park Walk
London, S.W.10.

Mr Alan Watkins,
The Observer,
8 St Andrews Hill,
London, E.C.4.

10th September 1979.

Dear Watkins,

To be blunt, I don't usually like your stuff. It's too clever by half, in my opinion, and your tone - at once 'superior' and colloquial - often grates.

However, in your obituary for Philip Hope-Wallace this Sunday you hit an appropriate note for once. Well done!

It so happens that I have recently commissioned myself to compile an anthology of modern British prose and I would like your permission to quote two passages from your piece as under:

'Philip Hope-Wallace, opera critic of 'The Guardian', died last week. He was 67. He was an essayist, a linguist, a drinker and a wit.....He was beautifully polite - as much to a West Indian bus conductor as to his host at a party, to whom he would invariably send a thank-you letter.'

Of how many people, in these confusing times, can one say that they are polite to West Indian bus conductors? Precious few, alas! What a great man he must have been!

The other passage I would like to use is:

'He was once discussing the prologue to 'Pagliacci' on the wireless. "When I cease being moved by that music," he said, "I shall know I am dead". It is difficult to think of any young music critic today who could or would make that kind of statement'.

It is indeed.

His anecdote, about Elsie and Doris Waters, which you quote, is certainly hilarious. 'It is a measure of his gifts as a racon- teur,' you wrote, 'that it never failed to bring the house down'. I'm not surprised. I'm still chuckling over it myself.

I look forward to receiving the necessary permissions.

Yours sincerely,

Henry Root.

Henry Root.

THE OBSERVER

The Observer Limited Registered number 146482 England
Registered office 8 St. Andrews Hill London EC4V 5JA Telephone 01-236 0202
Telegrams Observer London EC4 Telex 888963

22nd September 1979

Mr H. Root,
139 Elm Park Mansions,
Park Walk,
London SW10

Dear Mr Root,

Thank you for your letter of 10th September.
I apologise for the delay in replying.
Reproduction of my articles is in the hands
of my agent, Giles Gordon, Anthony Sheil
Associates Ltd., 2/3 Morwell Street, London
WC1, with whom I suggest you get in touch.

Yours sincerely,

A. Watkins

Alan Watkins

139 Elm Park Mansions
Park Walk
London, S.W.10.

The Chairman,
Leslie & Godwin,
Dunster House,
Mark Lane,
London, E.C.4.   12th September 1979.

Dear Sir,

Your name has been given to me as insurance brokers who
are more or less on the up and up, paying their obligations
without demur.

I am planning to take a late summer holiday with Mrs Root
and my two youngsters, Doreen (20) and Henry Jr (15), on the
sunshine island of Ibiza.

Having never trusted foreigners since being overcharged in
Llandeilo, I write now to enquire about cover for the trip.

What would be the cost of insuring myself, Mrs Root and
my two youngsters against seizure from the beach and ransom?

I would pay generously in the case of myself and reasonably
for my two youngsters, but I would not wish the premiums on Mrs
Root to be too heavy. She's still a handsome woman, but no
longer in her first youth. Don't misunderstand me. It's not
that I wouldn't pay to get her back. It's simply hard to credit
that anyone would snatch her in the first place - so why waste
money on a large premium?

Perhaps you could send round one of your young operatives
with the kidnap application forms.

Yours faithfully,

Henry Root

Henry Root.

Leslie & Godwin Overseas (Non Marine) Ltd

SUBSIDIARY OF LESLIE & GODWIN LTD.
LLOYD'S INSURANCE BROKERS

Dunster House
Mark Lane
London EC3P 3AD (Reg. Office)

Telex **888581** LESGO.G
Cables
Twentythree London
Telephone 01 623 4631

Registered No. 1401861 England

Mr.H.Root,
139 Elm Park Mansions,
Park Walk,
LONDON, S.W.10.

19th September 1979

Our Reference JD/CC

Dear Sir,

Thank you for your letter of 12th September enquiring about the availability of Kidnap and Ransom insurance. We have been arranging this class of business for clients for several years and for security reasons we have code named this insurance 'Porters'.

We enclose herewith an application form for 'Porters' insurance which we would ask you to complete and return to us as soon as possible. On receipt of the completed form we will endeavour to obtain a quotation for yourself and your family.

Thank you for your enquiry.

Yours faithfully,

for Manager.

139 Elm Park Mansions
Park Walk
London, S.W.10.

Mr Paul Johnson,
The Evening Standard,
47 Shoe Lane,
London, E.C.4.

12th September 1979.

Dear Johnson,

Your article in yesterday's 'Evening Standard' about the
proposed tour of this country by a party of South African rugby
players started a right old ding-dong in my lounge-room, I can
tell you!

I supported you whole-heartedly, of course, in your ringing
denunciation of the notion that the State should ever meddle in
the private arrangements of sportsmen on and off the ball, and I
vehemently seconded your telling point that rent-a-crowd lefties
who would ban all tours of this country by our Springbok friends
should, to be consistent, also oppose sporting engagements with
the Soviet Union, but my daughter Doreen expostulated as follows:

"Johnson's talking through his hat as usual. An act util-
itarian - which is what most of us are - is not involving himself
in a contradiction (in any formal sense) if he opposes sporting
links with South Africa but not with the Soviet Union. Anyway,
protesting against the South African rugby players is not a political gesture, but a moral one. What old-fashioned deontologists,
like Johnson, are in fact saying is 'keep morality out of sport'.
To be consistent they should campaign for the legalisation of
cock-fighting, bear-baiting and wrestling in mud by naked mountain
ladies, all of which are considered sports by certain people."

Well, I don't understand what she's talking about, so perhaps
you'd like to answer her. I'm sure she must be mistaken and I'd
like to be able to point out the fallacy in her position. Could
you oblige? I'd be most grateful.

I look forward to hearing from you.

Up the Springboks!

Yours sincerely,

Henry Root

Henry Root.

PAUL JOHNSON, Copthall, Iver, Buckinghamshire. Iver 653350

11 Oct 79

Nothing I can say like have the
slightest influence on a socialist
student at Essex University. No doubt,
I won't try. Someday, will emerge from
your daughter will emerge from
under the carapace of her jargon
a begin to think for herself. P.J.

139 Elm Park Mansions
Park Walk
London, S.W.10.

Mr Ray Cooney,
26 Charing Cross Road,
London, W.C.2.   15th September 1979.

Dear Cooney,

      I see you're reviving Carol Channing at Drury Lane. Well
done!

      She's a game old bat and can always be heard at the back of
the hall. Of how many of today's young artistes can that be said?

      I was disappointed not to receive an answer from you to my
letter of 29th March, in which I suggested that I might become one
of your fairies. Perhaps you never received it. In case that is
so, I now enclose a copy.

      I'd like to bring Mrs Root and my two youngsters, Doreen (20)
and Henry Jr (15) to Miss Channing's first night on 25th September.
I know you'll want to issue me with complimentary tickets (as a
potential fairy), but I wouldn't hear of it. Here's a fiver for
yourself. Send me four of your best orchestra stalls.

      Are you having a 'do' afterwards? Let me know where it's
being held as I'd like Mrs Root to meet Miss Channing.

      See you on the 25th!

      Good luck!

      Henry Root

      Henry Root.

P.S. I'd really like to invest in your shows, so send me a prospectus
of your up-coming productions. Cheers!

139 Elm Park Mansions
Park Walk
London, S.W.10.

Lord Thorneycroft,
Conservative Party Central Office,
32 Smith Square,
London, S.W.1.   12th September 1979.

Dear Lord Thorneycroft,
          Following a most unsatisfactory exchange of letters with two
of your jacks-in-office at HQ - Major-General Wyldbore-Smith and
Mr Alistair McAlpine - I was compelled to write to the Liberal Party
yesterday, informing them that I intended to join their ranks.

          Word of this apparent defection will by now have reached you.
Don't worry. I'm only pretending to join the Liberals for the purposes of a life peerage. (Titles, as you no doubt know, come at a
sharper price from them, due to their lack of current wherewithall.)
The purpose of this letter is to emphasise that I will, of course,
remain at heart a Tory, and as soon as I am adequately ennobled will
once more cross the floor.

          Meanwhile I can be of use to you as a mole in their midst,
attending confabs wired for sound and reporting back to you on
weirdos bent on direct action and civil disobedience.

          For the moment I think we should keep this arrangement con-
fidential between ourselves. Better that our Leader should remain
uncompromised. Were a wheel to come off it would be better that
she was genuinely uncognisant of the fact that her man-on-the-doorstep
had become a 'plumber'.

          I enclose a pound for yourself as a token of my essential
loyalty.

          Support Mrs Thatcher!

          Over and out!

          Henry Root.

Henry Root.

CONSERVATIVE & UNIONIST CENTRAL OFFICE,
32 SMITH SQUARE,
WESTMINSTER, SW1P 3HH,

Telephone: 01-222 9000

PT/SO   4th October, 1979

Dear Mr Root,

Lord Thorneycroft has asked me to thank
you for your letter of the 12th September,
the contents of which he has noted.

He has asked me to return to you herewith
your £1.

Yours sincerely,

Shirley Oxenbury
Chairman's Office

H. Root, Esq.,

139 Elm Park Mansions
Park Walk
London, S.W.10.

Mr And Peter Forster,
The Evening Standard,
47 Shoe Lane,
London, E.C.4.   21st September 1979.

Dear Mr And Peter Forster,

        In your column yesterday you asked how the expression
'Hampstead intellectual' came into being.

        Had you lived in this country a little longer you would
know that the term dates from the time that Mr Hugh Gaitskill
(who used to be the leader of the Labour Party here) lived in
this part of London. It was his custom to hold early evening
sherry parties in his home for so-called left-wing 'thinkers'
of his stripe. Most had been to Winchester School and had
acquired their leanings through being kicked hard and often
at an impressionable age by the likes of better adjusted Winchester boys such as Mr Willie Whitehouse.

        Had you lived among us for a little longer you would also
know that it is customary in this country to reply to letters.
I have not yet heard from you in response to mine of 6th September.

        Never mind. Here's a stamp. In fact, here are two stamps.
Now you can answer both my letters.

        I hope you are gradually becoming more accustomed to our
ways. We're not a difficult people if treated with respect. Good
luck to you!

        Jeres!

Henry Root

Henry Root.

139 Elm Park Mansions
Park Walk
London, S.W.10.

The President,
The Society of West End Theatre Managers,
19 Charing Cross Road,
London, W.C.2.   27th September 1979.

Mr President,

    I wish to protest in the strongest possible terms about the
behaviour of one of your members.

    On the 15th of this month I sent Mr Ray Cooney a fiver and
instructed him to send me four front stalls for the revival of
Carol Channing at Drury Lane.

    I haven't heard a word from him! I didn't receive my tickets
and no doubt the fiver's down the drain!

    I realise that Mr Cooney, being, I take it, a recent immigrant
to this country, may not as yet be fully au fait with our way of
doing things, but I think you'll agree with me that simply pocketing
a fellow's money probably isn't on even where Cooney comes from.

    I may add that I wrote to Cooney originally in April saying
that I'd like to be a fairy in one of his shows, and he didn't answer
that letter either!

    His kind have delightfully sunny and easy-going temperaments,
of course, but I think there is a limit to the allowances one can
go on making. I look forward to hearing what action you propose to
take against him, Mr President, and to receiving my money back.

    Yours sincerely,

    Henry Root

    He

ray cooney productions limited

SUITE 33, 26 CHARING CROSS ROAD, LONDON WC2H 0DH
Telegraphic Address: RAYCOPRODS LONDON   Telephone: 01-240 3747
                                                              01-836 9771
V.A.T. Regn. No. 239 5344 46   01-836 9751

                    3 October 1979

                    Henry Root Esq.
                    139 Elm Park Mansions
                    Park Walk
                    LONDON, S.W.10.

Dear Mr. Root,

We are in receipt of your letter dated 15 September
which unfortunately only reached this office yesterday.
We are therefore returning your £5 which you enclosed
as the first night of Miss Channing at Drury Lane has
since come and gone.

Yours sincerely,

for Ray Cooney

139 Elm Park Mansions
Park Walk
London, S.W.10.

Lord Rothermere,
Associated Newspapers Ltd,
Carmelite House,
London, E.C.4.

16th September 1979
Battle of Britain Sunday!

Dear Lord Rothermere,

What a day to be writing to you! Battle of Britain Sunday!
I believe you flew Spitfires in the last show. Or was that Sir
Max Atkins? Same difference. Well done!

I read recently that you are being sued for libel by your
scandal writer, Nigel Dempster. It seems you compared the flavour
of his column to that of stale cabbage. That's been obvious to
one and all for years. Why have you only just caught on? Never
mind. You probably don't read 'The Daily Mail' and who shall blame
you?

I see that a friend of Dempster's, the little Jap Mr Taki,
attacks you in this week's 'Spectator' on the grounds that your
father was crackers and ran his affairs from a pigeon loft. So
what? The least said about Dempster's father the better, I imagine,
and no doubt at the time you were flying Spitfires over the White
Cliffs of Dover Mr Taki's father was bombing Pearl Harbour. So
where would they have been on VD Day? Lying low, I wouldn't wonder!

Anyway, I'm glad to see you're defending the action. You'll
win hands down, of course, but I enclose a pound to help with the
costs.

Might I suggest alternative defences?

1.   <u>Nothing</u> said about Dempster could lower him in the estimation
of right-thinking folk on the Clapham omnibus. Or:

B.   'The Daily Mail' is held in such low repute that nothing in
it could be believed, least of all anything said by its proprietor.

Let's go!

Yours sincerely,

Henry Root

Henry Root.

THE CHAIRMAN'S OFFICE

ASSOCIATED NEWSPAPERS GROUP LIMITED

NEW CARMELITE HOUSE,
CARMELITE STREET,
LONDON, EC4Y 0JA

TELEPHONE
01-353 6000
01-353 4000
TELEX 261461/2

4th October, 1979

Mr. Henry Root,
139 Elm Park Mansions,
Park Walk,
London S.W. 10.

Dear Mr. Root,

I have great pleasure in returning your pound as I am not being sued for libel by Mr. Nigel Dempster.

From your letter it would seem that you are addicted to the reading of idle gossip and are foolish enough to believe all that you read. It is a pity that apparently an expensive education should have been so wasted.

Yours sincerely,

M White

pp Lord Rothermere.

Dictated by Lord Rothermere.
Signed in his absence.

Registered Office, Carmelite House, London, EC4Y 0JA Reg. No. 84121 England

139 Elm Park Mansions
Park Walk
London, S.W.10.

Dr John Rae,
Westminster School,
17 Dean's Yard,
London, S.W.1.   17th September 1979.

Dear Dr Rae,

I would like to congratulate you on the well produced TV
commercial for your school last week. You won't mind my saying,
however, that you yourself came across as a bit of a ponce,
putting yourself about the quad in red robes of a flowing cut
and declaiming your lines like King Rat in a pantomime. Mrs
Root explained that such behaviour comes under the heading of
'tradition' and dates from Uncle Tom's Schooldays. I expect you
know what you're doing.

Here's the heart of it. I've had a lot of trouble over the
years with my boy, Henry Jr, and I might be interested in seeing
whether you can straighten him out. First I'd have to be satisfied
on certain points arising out of the commercial. On the debit
side we have to put your own performance; the information imparted
that the fat foreign raconteur Peter Ustinov is a former pupil as
are 'Tony' Benn and Philby the Foreign Office mole; the emphasis
on book-learning rather than ball games; the participation of girls
in the curriculum; the fact that an older lad was clearly seen at
one point to be playing the guitar; and the apparent discontinuation
of corporal punishments.

I was favourably impressed, however, by your firm stand
against the use of drugs obtained from ethnic minorities in the
town and still more by the fact that you encourage the taking of
alcohol so long as the lads are resourceful enough not to get
caught blotto. It seems too that you have already produced six
Prime Ministers. Well done! This suggests that the masters must
be a shade less obviously crackers than they look.

In the circumstances, and on balance, I'll take a risk with
my boy's future. I gather places are at a premium, so I'm prepared
to pay over the odds to secure him a position at the head of the
queue. I enclose a fiver (this is for you personally, you understand)
and I can tell you that there's a lot more where this came from if
you play your cards right.

I look forward to hearing from you.

Yours sincerely,

Henry Root

Henry Root.

THE HEAD MASTER
WESTMINSTER SCHOOL
17 DEAN'S YARD, SW1P 3PB
01-222 6904

18th September 1979

Dear Mr. Root,

Thank you for your letter of 17th September.

If you would like your son to be registered for Westminster you should write to the Registrar, Mr. Geoffrey Shepherd, Westminster School, Little Dean's Yard, London, S.W.1., or telephone him on 222 5516.   The entrance to Westminster is by examination only.

I am returning your £5 note; you will no doubt appreciate that I am not in a position to keep it.

Yours sincerely,

Mr. Henry Root,
139 Elm Park Mansions,
Park Walk,
London, S.W. 10.

139 Elm Park Mansions
Park Walk
London, S.W.10.

The Managing Director,
J. Walter Thompson Ltd,
40 Berkeley Square,
London, W.1.   17th September 1979.

Dear Sir,

No doubt you will have already been tipped off through the 'media' grapevine that Sidgwick & Jackson is shortly to publish Vol 1 in my series SEMINAL IDEAS IN A NUTSHELL, edited by HENRY ROOT with the assistance of Doreen Root (20).

For literary folk they seem to be more or less on the up and up (though a tendency to wear pink shirts, drop names and offer sherry wine at tea-time has to be watched) and doubtless they know how to evaluate a manuscript. Judging by what I've seen, however, (and in spite of the reasonable selling job they did for Shirley Conran, the cook, and Mr Edward Heath) I'm much less happy about their ability to push the product. The head of publicity is a girl (which hardly inspires confidence, I think you'll agree), two of the Directors, Stephen du Sautoy and Rocco Forte, are, as their names suggest, of foreign extraction, and already many of my most valid concepts - such as engaging 'Sir' Robert Mark to endorse the package on TV (television) - have been vetoed by some character who wafts into the office at lunchtime, sugars off moments thereafter for an 'appointment' in the West End and isn't seen again for the rest of the day.

In a word, they don't know how to hood-wink the paying customer into forking out for a product he didn't want in the first place.

This is where you come in. Bamboozling the mugs is your business. I've had my people run you through the computer and I'm glad to be able to tell you that you've come up brand new. Well done! In the circumstances I'm prepared to put the marketing of the series your way. (In fact I was strongly advised to give the job to young Bell of Saatchi and Saatchi, but it seemed un- patriotic to brief a Japanese outfit. Nothing racist, mind - I just don't draw too well with the clever little monkeys.)

When shall we meet to run a few ideas up the flag-pole? What about one day next week? If I hear nothing to the contrary, I'll run through the door of your office at 12.30 on Thursday 27th September.

Perhaps I should emphasise that I expect this account to be handled by you personally. I don't want to be greeted on the 27th by a junior visualiser or the lad who holds up the story- boards at a client's meeting!

Here's a pound. Come up with some solid, viable ideas and you'll find there's plenty more where this came from.

I'm looking for maximum visibility. So spend! Spend! Spend! This could be a valuable account for you.

Yours with a concept,

Henry Root

Henry Root.

J. WALTER THOMPSON COMPANY
LIMITED

40 Berkeley Square, London, W1X 6AD Tel: 01-629 9496
Telegraphic address: Thomertwal, London Telex: 22871

24th September 1979

Mr. H. Root
139 Elm Park Mansions
Park Walk
London SW10

Dear Mr. Root

Thank you so much for your letter.

Michael Cooper-Evans has passed it to me as the Account
Director of J. Walter Thompson's Entertainment Group.
I know that you were most anxious that you dealt with
him personally but he felt that such an exciting project
as yours should be handled by the appropriate department.

One thing I must explain is the way in which we get paid.
Occasionally we have fee payments, particularly on smaller
or development jobs, but mainly we take a commission on
the media expenditure. This is 15%. As an example I'm
returning 85p of your pound.

I'm looking forward to meeting you on Thursday, and perhaps
even Doreen.

Yours sincerely

SEAN O'CONNOR
Story-board Holder

DIRECTORS: J. J. D. Bullmore (*Chairman*), P. H. Miles, A. R. G. Morrison (*Deputy Chairmen*), M. Cooper-Evans, (*Managing Director*);
P. W. Bostock, I. N. E. Bruce, L. A. Carter, D. R. Cawston, M. W. M. Colebrook, D. R. M. Curling, G. W. Effer, J. B. H. Goble, T. S. Hamaton,
R. P. Hornby, B. H. C. Johnson, S. H. M. King, D. G. Lanigan, J. M. Lannon, G. J. Lawrence, G. J. S. Ogden, J. R. Page, J. A. Paine,
D. J. L. Richardson, D. E. A. Rousell, A. J. Scouller, A. W. Stead.

Registered Office: 40 Berkeley Square, London, W1. Registered in England No. 1190652.

139 Elm Park Mansions
Park Walk
London, S.W.10.

Mrs Deborah Owen,
78 Marrow Street,   19th September 1979.
Limehouse,
London, E.14.

Dear Mrs Owen,
        I enclose for your evaluation a copy of my humorous play
THE ENGLISH WAY OF DOING THINGS by HENRY ROOT. It's an amusing
romp in two acts with only enough unnecessary nudity to attract
the mugs.
        As you will quickly perceive, it concerns the antics of a
Police Commissioner from the north who is impeded in the course
of his duty by the fact that he is always socially out of his
depth with those whom he sets out to apprehend. I have based it
on the famous 'Spaghetti House Siege Situation', which, as you
will remember, dragged on for several days because when Sir Robert
Mark turned up with his handcuffs and a megaphone he was denied
entry on the grounds that he hadn't booked a table and was un-
suitably dressed for Knightsbridge.
        In fact Sir Robert himself has already turned down the part
of the Police Commissioner on the grounds that he doesn't really
want to be an actor, but I will shortly be offering the part of
Lady Mark to Miss Hylda Baker. Miss Glenda Jackson might be
suitable for the part of the rough old boiler who 'takes an early
bath' in Act 1.
        My friend Jeffrey Archer speaks most highly of your capacities,
endorsing you as an agent on the up-and-up with editorial expertise
and separate client account. Well done! In the circumstances I'm
prepared to put the representation of my play in your hands for
a trial period.
        I'm a trifle concerned by your address. I myself was born
in the East End, but I made it my business to swim clear as soon
as I could. Never mind. Your corner of THE ENGLISH WAY OF DOING
THINGS by HENRY ROOT should enable you to make the move to a more
literary neck of the woods. Perhaps when we meet you should come
to me. There are quite a few folk in your part of the world still
nursing bruised ribs from the days when I was elbowing my way up
the ladder in wet fish. I wouldn't want to embarrass those with
whom I once hob-nobbed as equals by passing among them now in my
Rolls HR1 without a nod. I'm sure you'll understand.
        I trust your husband, so-called Dr Owen, isn't in charge of
your foreign rights department! No, I'm only joking! He did his
best.

        Yours sincerely,
        Henry Root
        Henry Root.

DEBORAH OWEN
LITERARY AGENT · 78 NARROW STREET
LIMEHOUSE · LONDON E14 8BP
TEL: 01-987 5119 CABLES: DEBOWEN LONDON E14

21st September 1979

Henry Root Esq
139 Elm Park Mansions
Park Walk
London SW10

Dear Mr Root,

Thank you for your letter of September the 19th enclosing
your play entitled THE ENGLISH WAY OF DOING THINGS.

I fear that I do not handle plays as they require quite a
different appraisal to fiction and this is not an art in
which I feel well-educated.

You may find it helpful to look at the list of agents in
the CASSELL AND PUBLISHERS ASSOCIATION DIRECTORY OF PUBLISHING.
This will tell you which agencies will consider plays and also
those that specialise in plays.

I am returning your play to you with this letter and thank
you for enclosing an s.a.e.

Yours sincerely,

Deborah Owen

Encl.

139 Elm Park Mansions
Park Walk
London, S.W.10.

Miss Harriet Harman,
The National Council for so-called Civil Liberties,   24th September 1979.
186 Charing Cross Road,
London, W.C.1.

Dear Miss Harman,
        I saw you on TV the other night arguing the matter of jury-
fixing with that foreign boffin from London University, Professor
Zander.

        Why should an attractive lass like you want to confuse her
pretty little head with complicated matters of politics, juris-
prudence, sociology and the so-called rights of citizens? Leave
such weighty considerations to us men, that's my advice to you!

        A pretty girl like you should have settled down by now with
a husband and a couple of kiddies. Or, if you must earn a living,
why do you not pursue a career suitable to women such as that of
model, actress, ballroom-dancing instructress or newsreader? You
certainly have the looks! (You will agree, I think, that the
outstanding success achieved by the misses Rippon and Ford has
amply demonstrated that reading the news is far too trivial an
occupation for grown men.)

        Here's a pound. Go out and buy a pretty dress and then give
my friend Lord Delfont a phone call. Mention my name and say you'd
like to drop in for some advice about a career in entertainment or
ATV.

        Good luck!

        Yours sincerely,

        Henry Root

        Henry Root.

139 Elm Park Mansions
Park Walk
London, S.W.10.

His Honour Judge King-Hamilton Q.C.
The Old Bailey,
London, E.C.4.   24th September 1979.

Your Honour,

So! Amid the predictable and orchestrated cries of outrage
from the so-called liberal press, 'The Guardian' has let the cat out
of the bag re the sensible practice of 'jury fixing'!

You were right to give 'The Guardian' a tongue-lashing from
the bench, but you might, in my opinion, have gone further. Did not
such outrageous irresponsibility warrant a night or two in the
sneezer for the Editor? I'm sure Mr Justice Cantley or Mr Justice
Melford Stevenson as was would have taken more drastic steps.

What, after all, is wrong with jury rigging? Only those who
have broken the law have anything to fear from this practice. And
what would be the point of the police taking endless trouble to
rig the evidence unless the jury had been tampered with too? Months
of valuable police work would go down the drain. This is what that
fine man Sir Robert Mark understood so well. He knew that the whole
point of a criminal trial is to get the defendant into what we call
'a no-win situation'.

Good luck with the anarchists trial which has given rise to
all the brouhaha. Is it too late for me to be appointed to the
new rigged jury? With me on the panel you'd have one vote of guilty
in your pocket before you started.

Might I congratulate you (better late than never!) on the fine
showing you put up while presiding last year at the so-called Gay
News blasphemy trial? Lemon should have gone to the slammer, but
otherwise you shaped up well and I trust your client Mrs Whitehouse
was appropriately grateful.

How about a signed photo? You've got the sort of head that
might put the wind up my boy, Henry Jr. The lad's badly off the
rails and your features on his bedroom wall might stop his thoughts
and hands straying whither they'd be better not to stray till later.

Tell me something. Are you merely Judge King-Hamilton rather
than Mr Justice King-Hamilton because you're no good at it, or is
there another reason?

Keep up the good work!

I look forward to hearing from you.

Yours sincerely,

Henry Root

Henry Root.

CENTRAL CRIMINAL COURT

Old Bailey London EC4M 7EH

Telephone 01-248 3277

	Your reference
	Our reference
	MM/MJG
	Date
	25 September 1979

Dear Mr. Root,

    I write on behalf of His Honour Judge King-Hamilton to acknowledge receipt of your letter dated 24th September, addressed to him.

    As I am sure you are aware, Her Majesty's Judges are not permitted to enter into personal correspondence relating to cases which they are trying nor, indeed, to make comments publicly about them but the Judge has asked me to thank you for your interest in writing to him.

            Yours sincerely,

Michael McKenzie
Courts Administrator

H. Root Esq.,
139 Elm Park Mansions,
Park Walk,
London, S.W.10.

139 Elm Park Mansions
Park Walk
London, S.W.10.

The Senior Treasury Counsel,
The Old Bailey,
London, E.C.4.   24th September 1979.

Dear Sir,

　　　Now that the sensible practice of 'jury fixing' is out in
the open thanks to the irresponsible behaviour of 'The Guardian',
I would like to nominate myself as 'a rigged juryman' in certain
trials.

　　　In cases involving pornographers, blasphemers and those prone
to civil agitation and disorder you'd have at least one vote under
your belt even before the curtain had gone up.

　　　I am 45, a householder, a man of means and not without associates, including Sir James Goldsmith.

　　　You can rely on me!

　　　Here's a pound! Put my name at the top of the list if you
want a conviction!

　　　I look forward to hearing from you.

　　　Yours sincerely,

　　　Henry Root

　　　Henry Root.

Copies to:　The Lord Chancellor.
　　　　　　 The Attorney-General.
　　　　　　 The DPP.

CENTRAL CRIMINAL COURT
Old Bailey London EC4M 7EH

Telephone 01-248 3277

Your reference

Our reference 013/MS/GO

Date
28 September 1979

Dear Sir,

　　　Thank you for your letter of 24th September,
the contents of which have been noted.

　　　I am returning your £1 note.

　　　　　　　Yours faithfully,

　　　　　　 for Courts Administrator

Mr. Henry Root,
139 Elm Park Mansions,
Park Walk,
London.
S.W.10

139 Elm Park Mansions
Park Walk
London, S.W.10.

Mr Malcolm Muggeridge,
c/o The Parkinson Show,
BBC TV,
London, W.12.   4th October 1979.

Dear Mr Muggeridge,

    Congratulations on your performance last night in 'The
Parkinson Show'! For once Parky met his intellectual equal.
Well done!

    That said, I must admit that my daughter Doreen (20) took
exception to some of your remarks. She found you particularly
unsound on the concept of progress. "It is an illusion", you
averred.

    "In denying the possibility of progress," my Doreen pro-
claimed, "Muggeridge seems to be using the word in a rather
unusual way. Perhaps he is confusing it with the notion of
perfectability. If he is merely arguing for fallibilism, then
of course I'd agree with him. However, if he's using the word
'progress' as it's generally used, then he would seem to be
talking nonsense - and not for the first time. For instance,
would he want to argue that he has made no progress as a writer
in the last sixty years? Does he deny the possibility of
improvement? If he thinks he's improved, then he must believe
in 'progress' as the word is commonly used. If he doesn't think
he's progressed at all, then I would suggest he doesn't understand
what the term means. If he would merely admit that while he
has made some progress he's still no bloody good and his entire
writing career has been a total waste of time, then of course
I'd agree in his case, while making greater claims for serious
writers".

    What do you say to that?

    I left the lounge-room to make tea at a certain point in the
show, so I missed the introduction of the third lady with mauve
hair swept up and rather too much personal jewellery here and there.
Surely this couldn't have been your wife, referred to by Parkinson
in the course of the show as beautiful and by yourself as delightful? If she is your wife, can't you stop her wearing gents' suits
in public? If she isn't your wife why on earth did you bring her
with you?

    Could I trouble you for a photo? I know you don't favour
personality cults and have testified to this in your many 'media'
appearances, but you are Mrs Root's favourite celebrity after
Terry Wogan and a photo of you would make her day. I enclose
the postage!

    Yours sincerely,

    Henry Root

    Henry Root.

139 Elm Park Mansions
Park Walk
London, S.W.10.

Derek F.S. Clogg Esq,
Theodore Goddard & Co,
16 St Martin's-le-Grand,
London, E.C.1.

4th October 1979.

Dear Mr Clogg,

Women are sentimental creatures, are they not? When they leave you, they like to hang on to something of yours they've grown attached to. Your money, your house, your cars, your children.

I write to you thus because, following an unfortunate lapse at 'The Talk of the Town' about which I'd rather talk in detail only in conference, I'm thinking of dumping Mrs Root. The mishap was occasioned by the fact that Mrs Root had recently seen a film of a wine-tasting festival on TV (BBC2) in which the participants had, after sampling for bouquet and after-taste, hit a spittoon from three yards. Taking this to be the done thing, Mrs Root took aim and hit the wine-waiter in the eye over the same distance. The fact is I'm after a peerage, and whoever's at my side as Lady Root must measure up.

I'm told that you're the top divorce lawyer in town, acting smartly for such as the Duchess of Argyle and the 'headless' Cabinet Minister who waited at table in a suspender-belt. Well done!

My concern is that I'm a very well-to-do man, duly alarmed by stories in the media of the large sums folk of substance now have to hand over to their wives on parting. Only this week I read that the wife of the cowboy Clint Eastwood is tearing into him to the tune of ten million!

Can we fix things so that Mrs Root only manages to pull away a few thousand? Do you have a scheme? She's welcome to the children.

When can we meet? What about Monday 15th October at noon? Perhaps we can discuss tactics over lunch.

I look forward to our first conference.

Yours sincerely,

Henry Root.

THEODORE GODDARD & CO.

16 ST. MARTIN'S-LE-GRAND
LONDON EC1A 4EJ

Telephone: 01-606 8855
Cables: Assumpsit London E.C.I
Telex: 884678
Telegrams: Assumpsit London Telex
Telecopier Extension 208
L.D.E. and C.D.E. Box Number 47
Stock Exchange Number STX 2346

D DUDLEY MORGAN
PETER A J MORLEY
J N FISHER
R DEREK FOX
BLANCHE H M A LUCAS
MARÉ N STACEY
MICHAEL Q WALTERS
F J CALDERAN
R K SHUTE
H J W TOD
EDWIN A JONES
WILLIAM S ROGERS
M A CROFT BAKER
M J HARRIS
ANTONY HEALD

CHRISTOPHER CLOGG
W H STUART MAY
ANDREW BINGHAM
MARTIN O CHESTER
P GRAFTON GREEN
DIANA GUY
DAVID S WILKINSON
R M PRESTON
DEREK W LEWIS
SIMON STUBBINGS
MARTIN KRAMER
GUY I F LEIGH
C J J MAPLES
DIANA SHEEZUM

Associate Offices:

167 RUE DE L'UNIVERSITE
PARIS 75007
Telephone: (010 331) 705 89 45
Telex: 250661

LAGASCA 106
MADRID 6
Telephone: (010 34 1) 275 03 24
Telegrams: Interlex

R DEREK WISE C.B.E. (RESIDENT IN PARIS)
EDWARD WILTSHIRE (RESIDENT IN MADRID)

CONSULTANT
DEREK F. S. CLOGG

ASSOCIATES   BRUCE S. WALTER

E. A. CLARKE
NICHOLAS WHITNEY

OSPREY HOUSE
5 OLD STREET
ST. HELIER, JERSEY C.I
Telephone (0534) 78065
Telex 4192289

Our Ref 5.

8th October 1979.

Dear Mr. Root,

Thank you for your letter of the 4th October.

I should be very happy to see you to discuss your case, but I am starting an action today which will last about three weeks and I should not be able to see you except at 4.30 or thereabouts in the afternoon. Perhaps you could kindly telephone my secretary and make an appointment.

Perhaps I ought to tell you our terms of business. My time is charged out at £50 an hour. My assistants at about £35, and before starting any litigation we have to be put in funds to the extent of £500 generally on account of our costs and disbursements such as Counsel's fees etc.

Yours sincerely,

Derek F.S. Clogg.

Henry Root, Esq.,
139 Elm Park Mansions,
Park Walk,
London SW10.

139 Elm Park Mansions
Park Walk
London, S.W.10.

Derek F.S. Clogg Esq,
Theodore Goddard & Co,
16 St Martin's-le-Grand,
London, E.C.1.

9th October 1979.

Dear Mr Clogg,

Thank you for your letter of 8th October in the matter of dumping Mrs Root. I note your charges and those of your assistant and would say that both seem reasonable.

It so happens that since I wrote to you on 4th October I have had a slight change of heart. This has been brought about by my sudden realisation that Mrs Root is, after all, a solid wife and mother, who has often held up adequately in public bearing in mind her background (cocktail waitress) and the fact that two nights ago she carried out a random spot check of my personal parts (you know what women are like) and came across some photographs of an 'artistic' bent of some 'models' posing at a price. Though these photographs were legitimately taken in the course of my researches for a book commissioned by Jonathan Cape Ltd, Mrs Root has most sensibly persuaded me that they could be misconstrued in the wrong hands.

In the circumstances I judge it best to reconsider the marriage situation for the time being, though if matters deteriorate I will get in touch with your 'personal' secretary for a conference.

Meanwhile I compute that I have taken up, say, ten minutes of your valuable time and I accordingly enclose as per your tariff a fiver (cash! No problem with our friends at the Revenue!)

Yours sincerely,

Henry Root

Henry Root.

139 Elm Park Mansions
Park Walk
London, S.W.10.

Miss Mary Kenny,
The Sunday Telegraph,
135 Fleet Street,
London, E.C.4.

8th October 1979.

Dear Miss Kenny,
So! You have at last made the big leap from the obscurity of
the Women's Section to the centre pages where men of affairs like
Peregrine Worsthorne write!

Well done!

A small step for man. But a giant step for an Agony Aunt!

Your article this Sunday about the effeminacy of the Pope
was most interesting.

'The true man,' you wrote, 'is not permanently tough, agg-
ressive, granite-faced and unassailable; the true man is someone
who has the courage to be a whole individual, which **means developing**
his "feminine", emotional, spiritual side too.'

This is well said, but I wonder where you'd draw the line.
Take the case of my boy, Henry Jr (15). He has developed his feminine side to such an extent that it's difficult, in my opinion,
to know which sex he is.

He wears eye make-up and girl's hats, he pouts and sulks if
reprimanded, he sleeps in his earrings and shows no interest at all
in such normal masculine pursuits as pin-ups and sport.

Should one let **him develop** in his **own way, or should one**
thrash the lad?

I very much look forward to receiving your advice in this
matter.

Yours sincerely,

Henry Root

Henry Root.

13.10.79.

Dear Mr Root,

Thank you for your kind letter.
I suppose I should have said in
my piece that the "true man"
also develops his masculine
side — I rather took that for
granted : wrongly, actually. I
certainly would draw the line at
exaggerated behaviour in either

sex — especially behaviour exaggerat-
ing the characteristics of the other
sex. I think one should put
one's foot down, gently but
firmly — he probably would
react badly to an over-
tough approach.

Wishing you the best of
luck : my old Irish mother
still says "spare the rod"... Regards,
Mary K.

139 Elm Park Mansions
Park Walk
London, S.W.10.

Miss Marjorie Proops,
The Daily Mirror,
Holborn Circus,
London, E.C.1.

5th October 1979.

Dear Marje,

Mrs Root recently drew my attention to a back number of
'The Guardian' (left behind by a house-painter with a degree in
Psychiatry from Sussex University who was doing our lounge-room
in over-all muffin) in which a Miss Polly Twaddle argued that
wives should be paid a good wage for cleaning, hoovering, dusting,
making beds, cooking, shopping, sewing, darning, taking the
kiddies to school and spending long hours at the hair-dresser.

Good heavens! If I had to <u>pay</u> to have such trivial tasks
performed, I'd hire a man and have them done properly.

You look like a wise old bird. Do you agree?

Yours,

Henry Root.

Mirror Group Newspapers Limited

Holborn Circus London EC1P 1DQ
Switchboard: 01-353 0246

Telegrams: Mirror London EC1
Telex: 27286

Please Quote:-GM/62009/RL
From Marjorie Proops

Mr. H. Root,
139, Elm Park Mansions,
Park Walk,
London.S.W.10.

19th October,1979.

Dear Mr. Root,

Thank you for your letter which I read with interest.

Arguments both for and against payment to wives for housework can be very
persuasive but looking at things from a purely practical point of view I
don't think it is really feasible. After all - a man's wage provides the
economic base of maintaining the family unit and only an eccentric sort of
man would insist on spending his income solely on himself. Likewise, a housewife
who insisted on a " wage" for herself is not being very sensible because surely
a good and loving marriage is based on sharing everything and not upon cold
and hard financial bargaining.

I hope that my comments have answered your question.

With all good wishes to you and your wife.

Yours sincerely,

P.P MARJORIE PROOPS.

Marje Proops is away
so this letter is being
signed in her absence

Registered Office: Holborn Circus London EC1
A Company registered in England (No 168 660)
and a subsidiary of Reed International Limited

139 Elm Park Mansions,
Park Walk,
London, S.W.10

From: Lord Root
Chairman & Chief Executive
Henry Root Wet Fish

9th October 1979.

George Gale Esq,
The Daily Express,
Fleet Street,
London, E.C.4.

Dear Mr Gale,

I expect to be raised to the peerage in the near future and have therefore taken the precaution of having my new stationary printed in good time.

You will notice almost at once that I have utilised at the foot of the page one of your most telling pronouncements - a slogan which, if I may say so, encapsulates Tory thinking in a nutshell.

Well done!

It has been drawn to my attention, however, by my lawyers, Theodore Goddard & Co, that the use and publication of this without your permission could be considered a breach of copyright. They have suggested, therefore, that to be on the safe side I should write to you seeking the necessary permissions.

I should be most grateful to know that such permissions will be forthcoming.

Might I take this opportunity to congratulate you on your many fine polemical articles in 'The Daily Express'? You must be making quite a reputation for yourself and will no doubt soon be in a position to move on to a 'quality' paper such as 'The Daily Mail'. In the meantime 'The Express' can boast that in you and Jean Rook it has the two best writers in Fleet Street on the staff.

Well done!

Yours sincerely,

Henry Root

Henry Root.

Copy to Derek F.S. Clogg Esq, Theodore Goddard & Co.

"Common sense is a sturdy plant and self-interest a great fertiliser". George Gale

D5 ALBANY
PICCADILLY
LONDON W1V 9RG
01-734 4282

December 14 1979

Dear Henry Root,

Many thanks for the
down payment. I decided it
was neither bribery nor corruption
so spent it on champagne at
El [?] Vino's.

By all means use the
quote. I hope it sells
not just like hot cakes.

Yours sincerely,

George Gale.

139 Elm Park Mansions
Park Walk
London, S.W.10.

Mr Francis King,
The Spectator,
56 Doughty Street,
London, W.C.1.

9th October 1979.

Dear Mr King,

I am presently compiling an anthology of great modern British prose and I would like permission to include in it the opening paragraph of your book review in 'The Spectator' of 22nd September as under:

'We all have lists of things that, though there is nothing intrinsically wrong with them, just happen not to be to our tastes. My own list would include restaurants in which the service is better than the food and the decor than either; cars, however large or powerful, with only two doors; ocean cruises; and literary fantasies. The last of these aversions makes it impossible for me fully to enjoy 'Orlando', 'Lady into Fox' or 'The Master and Margarita', much though I admire Virginia Woolf, David Garnett and Mikhail Bulgakov; and it also makes it difficult for me to be sure of being fair to 'Wild Nights', much though I admire Emma Tennant too'.

This is how criticism should be, and so rarely is. Poised, urbane, civilised and always hinting at interests outside the musty world of books. Well done! As my daughter Doreen (20) said when she read it:

"Literary journalism of this distinction makes one realise that Dr Leavis died in vain".

I enclose a stamped addressed envelope for the courtesy of your permission or for the name and address of your accredited representative should you prefer to be handled by others.

I look forward to hearing from you.

Yours sincerely,

Henry Root

Henry Root.

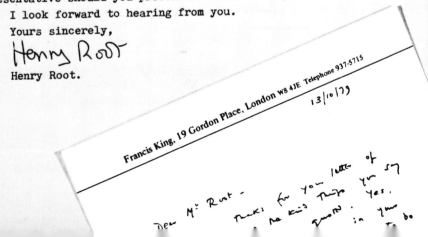

Francis King, 19 Gordon Place, London W8 4JE. Telephone 937-5715

13/10/79

Dear Mr Root -

Thanks for your letter of 57
the kind things you
quoted in your
to be

139 Elm Park Mansions
Park Walk
London, S.W.10.

Mr Victor Matthews,
Trafalgar House Investments Ltd,
1 Berkeley Street,
London, W.1.   16th October 1979.

Dear Mr Matthews,

I gather you own 'The Evening Standard'. Well done! It
makes a vital contribution to the artistic life of London - or
so it always claims. Nothing wrong with that.

It surprises me, however, that you don't encourage your
jounalists to reply to letters from ordinary folk on pertinent
issues. Surely intercourse between journalist and reader is the
life-blood of a popular newspaper?

On 6th September I wrote to your occasional columinist from
Norway, Mr And Peter Forster, congratulating him on the way he has
settled in among us, but chiding him for his suggestion that we
should all carry identity cards so that the police might more
easily distinguish between residents and tourists.

It's not in my nature to get anyone into trouble, but I have
to tell you that he didn't reply. So, on 21st September I wrote
to him again, gently pointing out that in this country it was considered polite to reply to letters. And, to encourage him, as it
were, I enclosed two 10p stamps.

These he seems to have pocketed! One must make allowances
for newcomers, of course, but I doubt whether pocketing a fellow's
stamps is on even where Forster comes from.

As I say, I don't want to get the poor chap into trouble, but
could you take him to one side and mark his card?

I look forward to hearing from you and to receiving a reply
from Mr And Peter Forster on the burden of my two letters.

Yours sincerely,

Henry Root

Henry Root.

TRAFALGAR HOUSE LIMITED

1 BERKELEY STREET · LONDON · W1X 6NN

TELEPHONE: 01-499-9020
CABLES: TRALON G

TELEX: 21341

23rd October, 1979

H. Root, Esq.,
139 Elm Park Mansions,
Park Walk,
London, S.W.10.

Dear Mr. Root,

Thank you for your letter of the 16th instant the contents of which I have noted, and I am passing this on to the Editor of the EVENING STANDARD so that he may look into this.

Yours sincerely,

Victor Matthews,
Group Chief Executive
and Deputy Chairman.

Directors: Nigel Broackes (Chairman)   Victor Matthews (Deputy Chairman and Chief Executive)   E. W. Parker (Managing Director)
G. C. D'Arcy Biss   Sir Francis Sandilands, CBE   G. H. B. Carter   W. B. Slater, VRD   The Marquess of Tavistock
V. A. Grundy   P. R. Howell   H. W. A. Francis, CBE   D. J. Groom   D. M. Taylor
Registered Office: 1 Berkeley Street, London, W1X 6NN.   Company No. 867281   Registered in England.

**Evening
STANDARD**

P.O. Box 136 47 Shoe Lane LONDON EC4P 4DD

Telephone 01-353 8000 Telex 21909

From the Editor

26 October 1979

Dear Mr Root,

    Mr Victor Matthews has sent me your
letter of 16 October. I agree with you that
nothing is more infuriating than to write
a letter to someone requiring a reply and
to get nothing back, particularly when you've
enclosed stamps.

    Mr Forster is a freelance who is not on
my staff, but I have written asking him to
reply to your letter.

              Yours sincerely,

CHARLES WINTOUR

H Root Esq.,
139 Elm Park Mansions,
Park Walk,
London SW10.

EVENING STANDARD CO., LTD.

Registered Office 47 SHOE LANE LONDON EC4P 4DD   Registered London No 193452

139 Elm Park Mansions
Park Walk
London, S.W.10.

Mr Denis Thatcher,
10 Downing Street,
London, S.W.1.   18th September 1979.

Dear Thatcher,

As you will know, I have kept in close touch with the Prime
Minister, your wife, over the past few months, advising her as to
door-step opinion. She's a very busy woman, of course, so generally
some fellow called Ryder replies, but he seems a civil enough sort
of chap.

Anyway, it occurred to me today that she probably gets a lot
of letters and that it would make a nice change for you to find one
on your breakfast tray.

Incidentally, I'm much enjoying your correspondence now appearing in 'Private Eye', but one thing puzzles me. How do the letters
come into their possession? I can't believe that you've sold them
first serialisation rights, particularly since many of them seem to
touch on confidential matters. Surely there's a 'D' notice on all
the tippling that goes on at No 10, not least your own? Is there a
mole at HQ? Or have 'Private Eye' an operative who makes it his
business to introduce himself via a drain-pipe into your quarters
at a late hour for the purpose of going through your files? I'd
put little beyond them. My friend Sir James Goldsmith had a lot of
trouble with them. Did you know that at the time of his courageous
court case against them last year it was their custom to rummage
through his dustbins in search of discreditable scraps and droppings.

Perhaps you could advise me on a small matter. I'm of a mind
to join Deal Golf Club, of which I gather you're a member. In your
letter to your pal Bill published in the current 'Eye' you refer to
an incident involving a homosexualist treasurer who had his finger
in the till and elsewhere too I wouldn't wonder. Has this been sorted
out, and is the club now on a sound moral and financial footing? I
certainly don't want to enrol myself if there are still irregularities
upstairs at the 19th.

Keep up the good work! Your wife, Mrs Thatcher, is an inspirational leader and though you must sometimes tire of playing Yvonne
to her General de Gaulle, I'm sure your support is priceless.

I look forward to hearing from you, Denis.

Yours sincerely,

Henry Root

Henry Root.

1O DOWNING STREET

5th October 1979

Dear Mr. Root,

Mr Thatcher has asked me to reply to your letter of
18th September.

As an assiduous observer of and listener to
"door step opinion", which must necessarily occupy
a great deal of time, it may have escaped your
notice that "Private Eye" magazine has over
the years published several features (eg Mrs
Wilson's Diary and Heathco) which purported to
be authentic.   My researches have revealed
that they were simply imaginative figments
of journalistic enterprise.   The present
"correspondence" in the pillar of the publishing
establishment merely follows that tradition.

It therefore follows that your enquiry concerning
potential membership of a particular golf club might
more appropriately be made to the officers of the
club.

Yours sincerely,

Derek Howe

Derek Howe
Political Office

H Root Esq

139 Elm Park Mansions
Park Walk
London, S.W.10.

The Secretary,
Deal Golf Club,
Deal,
Kent.   10th October 1979.

Dear Sir,

I hereby nominate myself for membership of your well-run
club on the personal recommendation of Mr Denis Thatcher.

He tells me that you have managed to clear up the unpleasant-
ness you had involving a homosexualist treasurer with his hand
where it shouldn't have been and that a gentleman can now associate
himself publicly with your club without qualms.

Well done!

I gather that your greens are of the best and your bunkers
an adequate hazard off the tee. However, I should like to try them
out for myself and to this end I shall be arriving with Mrs Root
and my two youngsters, Doreen (20) and Henry Jr (15), for a round
before lunch on Sunday 28th October. Kindly ensure that there is
a space in your car park for my Rolls Royce HR1.

Neither Mrs Root nor I have essayed the game before, but we
are expensively equipped as to clubs and wardrobe. Do you hire
motorised buggies by the hour? Mrs Root has a leg, you understand,
and humping my new Gary Player specials round the course might
prove too much for her. (Don't worry! Whatever she may lack in
expertise out on the links, she'll more than compensate for by
her performance at the 19th! She was a cocktail waitress in her
younger days and can still sing twelve verses of 'Get off the
Table, Mabel, the Money's for the Beer!' with little prompting.)

Thatcher tells me that there's a queue of folk eager to
join your club in spite of the unfortunate publicity, so to encourage
you to leap-frog me up the waiting-list I now enclose a fiver for
yourself. No need to tell the rest of the Committee about your
windfall. They'll all want a 'drink'!

I look forward to meeting you on Sunday 28th October. Perhaps
you'd care to lunch with us? Bring your good lady, by all means,
but let's go dutch. I don't want to kick off with a large mess
bill!

Yours to the 19th!

Henry Root

Henry Root.

Secretary
F. W. Mullin
Telephone—Deal 4007

Royal Cinque Ports Golf Club Ltd.
Deal

Telephone   Deal
CLUB HOUSE   - 4328
PROFESSIONAL - 4170
CADDIE MASTER 4170

22nd October, 1979

H.Root, Esq.,
139, Elm Park Mansions,
Park Walk,
LONDON.S.W.10.

Dear Sir,

The Secretary of the Royal Cinque Ports Golf Club has passed to me your letter of 10th October.

I enclose herewith a cheque for £5.00 in return for the cash enclosed with your letter, which you sent as an inducement in order to enhance the possibility of being elected a Member of the Royal Cinque Ports Golf Club. The Secretary never has and never will be a party to this sort of financial inducement.

Yours faithfully,

GORDON C. TAYLOR
CAPTAIN

The Company is registered in England. No. 475915.
Registered Office: Royal Cinque Ports Golf Club, Golf Road, Deal, Kent CT14 6RF

139 Elm Park Mansions
Park Walk
London, S.W.10.

Mr Denis Thatcher,   24th October 1979.
10 Downing Street,
London, S.W.1.

Dear Thatcher,

Oh dear oh dear! I applied for membership of Deal Golf Club
as you suggested, and today I received this daft letter (copy enclosed)
from some silly old fool telling me that they can't accept financial
inducements!

Could you have a word with the old buffer next time you're
down there? Obviously the Secretary's got the stick by the wrong
end and I'm sending him a snorter today, but a stiff word from you
might clear the air.

Sorry to trouble you with this. Anything I can do for you,
just let me know.

Guess who I saw at 'The Bristol Suite' the other night? Old
'Tubby' Walton! I'd been first to the Embassy Club, where I'd had
the shock of my life. Remember it in the old days? Davy Kaye and
dancing partners who'd accept credit cards? Well, the place seems
to be under new management and the bunnies are now men! That's
right! I hadn't been there two minutes when some little fairy in
satin trunks asked me if I'd care to dance! Sign of the times, no
doubt. Anyway, I beat a hasty retreat and took myself off to 'The
Bristol Suite', where I saw old 'Tubby' Walton. He was as smashed
as a rat and under the table with a coloured 'hostess' who had a
ring through her nose. He'd just made her his sole beneficiary
under a new will he'd scribbled on a table-cloth. Should we tell
Peggy, do you think? Anyway, I told him about my experience at
'The Embassy' and he said:

"The Embassy, eh? That puts me in mind of a rum thing that
happened to me during the war. I had to go to Cairo on a diplomatic
mission and when I arrived at the airport I hailed a taxi and said
'Take me to the Embassy, Abdul.' Well, the confounded fellow took me
to some evil back-street establishment full of half-naked girls
smoking things through pipes and Guardsmen sodomising everything
that moved. 'No, no, no, Abdul!' I said. 'Not the British Embassy,
man, 'The Embassy Night Club'!! You have to watch these Arabs."

Rather odd, don't you think?

All the best,

Yours,

Henry Root

Henry Root.

139 Elm Park Mansions
Park Walk
London, S.W.10.

The Secretary,
The Royal Cinq Ports Golf Club,
Deal,
Kent.

24th October 1979.

Dear Mullin,

What's going on? I sent you a fiver to pop me to the top of
your waiting-list and now I've received an extraordinary letter
from some fellow called Taylor (who claims to be a Captain, though
whether Army or Royal Navy he doesn't say) returning the fiver and
pointing out that financial inducements aren't acceptable!

What's it got to do with him? I suppose he wants a fiver too.
Well that won't wash with me and I may say that Denis Thatcher, on
whose express recommendation I applied for membership, will not
be at all pleased by this development.

I now return the five pounds together with a copy of a letter
I have today sent Thatcher. He's got better things to do than be
troubled by this sort of cock-up, so pull your finger out, there's
a good fellow.

I look forward to receiving the membership application forms
by return.

See you at the 19th!
Yours sincerely,

Henry Root

Henry Root.

139 Elm Park Mansions
Park Walk
London, S.W.10.

Lord Snowdon,
22 Launceston Place,   15th October 1979.
London, W.8.

Dear Lord Snowdon,
        Here's a concept which could do us both a bit of good!
        Some months ago I was commissioned by Jonathan Cape Ltd to
produce a book entitled WOMAN WATCHING by HENRY ROOT. Far from
being a mere stroke of publishing opportunism, cashing in on the
rather dubious 'popular' success of 'Manwatching' by Desmond
Morris, this was to be a serious study of how women comport themselves in private places when supposing themselves to be unobserved.
        I went to work with Hasselblad and strobe, introducing myself
incognito when least expected, and, as you will see from the enclosed
photographs, obtained many telling angles before ejaculation.
        Imagine my surprise when, after an eternity of editorial
shadow-boxing and feminine dithering, Debra Byron (my editor at
Cape) withdrew from the project!
        Here's the scheme. It occurs to me that were the book to have
an Introduction by yourself one would be at an advantage when closing
a deal with another publisher, and the book on publication would
have a better chance of attracting the mugs to boot.
        I have in mind approximately 2000 well-chosen words by yourself,
for which I would pay handsomely. Perhaps you would prefer me to
tie up the details with your agent, if you have one. I myself, being
a businessman of various experiences not all to do with fish, represent myself to advantage, but you may prefer to be handled by
others. Nothing wrong with that.
        Might I congratulate you on your excellently designed monkey-
house at London Zoo? I was there on Saturday with my young nephew
Bruce (5) and was quite impressed. You couldn't see the monkeys,
but no doubt that was just as well. Not your fault.
        I look forward to hearing from you and I enclose a stamped
addressed envelope for the return of my prints after due scrutiny.
I wouldn't want to see them in 'Playboy' magazine under your name!

        Yours sincerely,

        Henry Root

        Henry Root.

23rd October, 1979.

Dear Mr. Root,

I am writing on behalf of
Lord Snowdon to thank you for your
letter of 15th October.

Although he appreciates the thought
which prompted you to write it is with
regret he is unable to take advantage
of your suggestion.

I enclose the photographs you kindly
sent with your letter.

Yours very sincerely,
Dorothy Everard
Personal Assistant to
The Earl of Snowdon.

Henry Root, Esq.

139 Elm Park Mansions
Park Walk
London, S.W.10.

Mrs Deborah Owen,
78 Marrow Street,
Limehouse,
London, E.14.

16th October 1979.

Dear Mrs Owen,

I'm so sorry I haven't replied sooner to your sensible letter of 21st September in which you were honest enough to point out that you knew nothing at all about the live theatre. Never mind. Your suggestion that you should represent me merely in the world of books suits me excellently, and I now enclose a synopsis of my work in progress — SEMINAL THINKERS IN A NUTSHELL, edited by HENRY ROOT — together with correspondence relating thereto between myself and the house of Sidgwick & Jackson.

From Lord Longford's letter you will see that his firm teetered on the very brink of buying the concept, only to gather up their skirts and draw back nervously like a silly girl startled by a mouse.

Before nominating another publisher, I thought I might pick your brains (you might as well earn your 5%!) What about Weidenfeld and Nicolson? Are you familiar with Lord Weidenfeld himself? I have always suspected that he might be my sort of person, but are they serious publishers? Or are they primarily in the catering business, occasionally celebrating a party by bringing out a book by a ballet critic, a titled pop historian or a dizzy Irish lady novelist with her head in the literary clouds and her mind on matters below the belt?

I look forward to hearing your reaction and I would like you to know how much more secure I feel about my literary future now that my affairs are to be responsibly represented.

Yours sincerely,

Henry Root

Henry Root.

DEBORAH OWEN
LITERARY AGENT · 78 NARROW STREET
LIMEHOUSE · LONDON E14 8BP
TEL: 01-987 5119 CABLES: DEBOWEN LONDON E14

22nd October 1979

Henry Root Esq
139 Elm Park Mansions
Park Walk
London SW10

Dear Mr Root,

I fear that you misunderstood my letter to you of September
the 21st.

I did write to you primarily to tell you that I do not
represent theatrical works but in fact I should also have
said that I am not taking on any new writers at the present
time. This is a very small agency and one of the realities
of staying small is that I have to accept the limitations
that this involves - ie: sticking to the number of authors
that I know I will have time to look after.

Therefore, I must thank you for your s.a.e. once again and
return to you your synopsis and letters.

Yours sincerely,

M. J. Dooling

Encls.

Deborah Owen Limited
Registered in England at the above address No. 1009342

139 Elm Park Mansions
Park Walk
London, S.W.10.

The Managing Director,
Robson Books,
28 Poland Street,
London, W.1.   25th October 1979.

Dear Sir,

       I have just returned from Selfridges department store where
I and Mrs Root attended a signing session held for 'David Jacobs's
Book of Celebrities' Jokes and Anecdotes', and I want you to know
that we're both still roaring with laughter at the amusing antics
of Mr Jacobs himself, Reggie Bosanquet, Arthur Mullard and Ernie
Wise! (Reggie seemed to have had a very good lunch! Let's hope
he's not reading the news tonight!)

       The book itself is a splendid rib-tickler and should do very
well as a stocking-filler for undemanding folk this Christmas. Well
done!

       What's more, it's given me this solid idea! Might not 'The
Book of Celebrities' Most Embarrassing Incidents' do even better?
I have in mind all those hilarious anecdotes 'personalities' recount
on 'chat' shows, usually involving matters appertaining to the
water-works in the case of men and, in the case of female celebrities, the collapse of their knicker elastic on formal occasions!

       Since the best of these anecdotes tend to be told on 'The
Parkinson Show', I think it might be a sharp idea to rope in
Michael as co-Editor. What do you think?

       I now enclose for your consideration a suggested list of
anecdotes and some of the celebrities we should invite to participate.

       I look forward to receiving the go-ahead to use your name.

       Yours sincerely,

       Henry Root

       Henry Root.

THE CELEBRITIES' BOOK OF EMBARRASSING INCIDENTS!

Edited by HENRY ROOT and Michael Parkinson.

Suggested anecdotes.

1.   The hilarious story recounted by Esther Rantzen on 'The Michael Parkinson Show' about the time she was drying her hair (stark naked!) in front of the gas fire in theatrical digs (this was when she was still a member of the general public). Someone (a man!) entered the room unexpectedly and was brought face to face with the sight of Esther's backside! (I can't remember all the hilarious details, but I'm writing to Esther today asking her to furnish me with same.)

2.   The incident involving that urbane actor Rex Harrison and the loose toilet seat! Harrison was at a smart showbiz party and had occasion to visit the loo! (It happens to all of us - even to celebrities!) Unbeknown to Rex, the loo seat was new and had not been properly fixed! He aimed a kick at the cat (which had accom-panied him uninvited into the smallest room!) and shot feet first through the door (he'd forgotten to lock it!), down the stairs, arriving like a man on a toboggan among the other celebrities in the lounge-room!

3.   The hilarious incident concerning David Niven and the missing Mess sherry! This occurred before Niven became a celebrity. He was still in the army at the time and was stationed in India. One evening the Colonel of Niven's regiment noticed that some of the best sherry was 'disappearing' and suspicion naturally fell on the darky mess-wallah. At Niven's suggestion, the bottle of sherry was passed round the table and the officers relieved themselves into it in turn! The next day more of the sherry had gone! So once again the irrepressible young officers filled it up by 'natural means'! This went on for a week or so. Then, concerned for the mess-wallah's health, they called him in and confronted him with the matter. It transpired that each evening he'd been putting a drop into the officers' soup!!

4.   The celebrated occasion when Diana 'Revolving' Dors went to a fancy-dress party as a hula-hula dancer from Hawaii and won first prize as a thatched cottage!

5.   The anecdote recounted by the lovely (and abrasively intelligent!) actress Diana Rigg (again on 'The Parkinson Show') about the first time she appeared nude on stage! She stepped nervously out of her clothes, whereupon a fellow in the front row of the stalls cried: "Get off! My girlfriend's got better boobs than that! Bring back the comic!"

6.   The hilarious occasion when that witty writer Katherine White-horn lost her knickers at Royal Ascot just as she was being presented to Her Majesty the Queen!

7.   The time when that exuberant, larger-than-life character, Oliver Reed went into a Turkish bath in the Fulham Road. He took off his clothes, piled them neatly in a corner and groped his way through

the steam to join the queue of men waiting to have a massage. Then the steam cleared and he discovered he was in a fish and chip shop! "What's it to be, madam?" enquired the proprietor, "cod or hake?"

9. The incident when Joan Collins stepped out of the bath, trod on her son's skate-board and shot out of the front-door and down the drive! If her money-belt hadn't got caught in the gate-post she'd have skated (nude!) down Old Church Street and into Kensington High Street, putting 2p onto the rates!

10. The incident involving Anna Raeburn and the Peeping Tom who gave himself up to the police!

11. The anecdote recounted by Terry Wogan about the men's relay race at the nudist camp! There was a mix-up with the baton at a change-over and one of the contestants was dragged half-way round the track!!

And many many more!

Ⓒ HENRY ROOT
139 Elm Park Mansions
Park Walk
London, S.W.10.

ROBSON BOOKS LIMITED
PUBLISHERS
28 Poland Street   London   W1V 3DB
Telephone   01-734 1052/3
Cables   Robsobook London W1

2nd November 1979

Mr Henry Root
139 Elm Park Mansions
Parl Walk
LONDON SW10

Dear Mr Root,

Than you for your letter and suggestion. Was Reggie Bosanquet really
present at Selfridges? If so, perhaps it was I who had the very good
lunch...........

On the face of it, it is a good idea but how would it differ from the
Book of Bricks? If it is really on a different tack, and Mr Parkinson
would agree to participate, then we could be interested. I see you
have his name on the top of the outline. Does this mean you have already
approached him? Perhaps you would be good enough to let me have your
thoughts —— and, also, it would be helpful to have some information
on your good self. At this stage, naturally we cannot give the go-ahead
to use our name.

I'll look forward to hearing from you.

Yours sincerely,

JEREMY ROBSON

Registered in England 1097826 Registered office as above Directors Jeremy Robson (Managing)

139 Elm Park Mansions
Park Walk
London, S.W.10.

Sir James Goldsmith,
Now!
161-189 City Road,
London, E.C.1.

21st October 1979.
Trafalgar Day! Let's Go!

Dear Sir James,

May I be the first to congratulate you on your excellent new
publication, NOW!? We needed a bang-up-to-the-minute news magazine
and NOW! fills the gap superbly. Your exclusive this week on the
sinking of the Titanic was especially timely. Well done!

I would also like to congratulate you on your balanced review
of 'Goldenballs', so-called Richard Ingrams's book about yourself.
That it is an ill-considered hotch-potch of lies, sneers and innu-
endoes comes as no surprise.

I gather the publishing trade is furious with you for reviewing
the book before its official publication day. How absurd! Why
should one wait - entirely to oblige a publisher - till publication
date to nail a slur? I believe, in fact, that you may have started
a viable new trend, which is to review books at any time, possibly
even before they are written. This would serve two purposes. An
adverse review might disuade an author from writing a worthless
work, whereas a rave notice would encourage him to go to his type-
writer.

It so happens that for some months I have been trying to
arrange publication of my own first novel - DAY OF RECKONING by
HENRY ROOT. From the enclosed copies of correspondence with the
house of Cape, together with the synopsis of the work, you will
see that it is a book of substance and that Cape were on the point
of publishing it when an attack of editorial cold feet caused them
to withdraw.

It occurs to me that were you (or someone else better qualified, nominated by your Literary Editor) to give the book a favour-
able review at this stage, another publisher might be persuaded to
take the book on.

I look forward to hearing from you.

Yours against conspirators in the media!

Henry Root

Henry Root.

TELEPHONE: 01-480 5676

65-68, LEADENHALL STREET.

LONDON.

EC3A 2BA.

26th October, 1979.

H. Root Esq.,
139 Elm Park Mansions,
Park Walk,
<u>LONDON S.W.10</u>.

Dear Mr. Root,

Thank you very much for your letter. Unfortunately we are not in the publishing *(of books)* business, so we cannot be of any direct help to you but I am sending your letter onto the Chief Executive of W. H. Allen to see whether he has any interest in your project. No doubt he will be in touch with you.

Yours sincerely,

<u>James Goldsmith</u>

139 Elm Park Mansions
Park Walk
London, S.W.10.

Mr Bruce Page,
The New Statesman,
10 Great Turnstile,
London, W.C.1.

23rd October 1979.

Dear Mr Page,

I hereby nominate myself for the post of Assistant Literary
Editor as advertised in recent issues.

Let me specify at once that I am not a regular reader of your
paper. However, my daughter Doreen (20) takes it for her sins, so I
have glanced through it often enough to see why you are eager to make
a clean sweep of your reviewing staff. The mistake of the present
incumbents is to review exclusively the work of so-called experts and
self-appointed cranks.

As was recently pointed out in a letter in your correspondence
columns by no less an authority than Alan Bennett (who, as you may
remember, was one of the four clever young dentists who took the town
by storm some years ago in the spoof review 'Beyond the Fringe'), the
only readable bits in your paper are now written by that comical old
party, Arthur Marshall. Hear! Hear!

It will be my policy as Deputy Literary Editor to recapture
readers lost to your more urbane competitor, 'The Spectator'. Like
the Literary Editor of that excellently civilised journal, I shall
select my reviewers for their knowledge of wine, haute cuisine, gaming,
cricket, blood sports and fisticuffs, and I will ensure that only
books of general interest - such as 'David Jacobs's Book of Celebrities'
Jokes and Anecdotes' - are covered. (Arthur Marshall would write
hilariously on this, but it's a smoked sprat to a porpoise that under
your present literary staff it won't even be reviewed.)

You'll want to know a little about me. Educated (like you, I
imagine) at the University of Real Life, I went early into the wet
fish business and, by keeping wages low and refusing to recognise
the unions, so flourished that I was able to retire to my corner a
few years ago. On the advice of my friend Jeffrey Archer (do you
know him, Bruce? Nice little man, bright as a button), I have now
turned my considerable energies to literary matters and my work in
progress includes: DAY OF RECKONING by HENRY ROOT, a novel rejected
by Cape; WOMAN WATCHING by HENRY ROOT, a psychological study of
women and madness (with an introduction by Lord Snowdon), commissioned
by Cape, but then rejected after much editorial dithering (photos
enclosed); and SEMINAL THINKERS IN A NUTSHELL, edited by HENRY ROOT.

I enclose synopses of these plus correspondence appertaining,
and I would be grateful if you would return them to me after due
scrutiny.

Let's smoke out the wet left and recapture the middle ground
from 'The Spectator'!

I look forward to meeting you, Bruce, and to discussing the
terms of my employment.

Yours sincerely,

Henry Root

Henry Root.

NEW STATESMAN

Registered Office:
10 Great Turnstile, London WC1V 7HJ
01-405 8471   Telex 28449
Cables: Newstat, London WC1

23 October 1979

Dear Henry Root,

In view of the large number of applications for
this post, I apologise for sending you a standard
reply informing you that unfortunately your
application was not successful. The new Deputy
Literary Editor will be Paul Binding.

Yours sincerely,

David Caute
Literary Editor

The Statesman
Reg
man: Richard Hoggart.   Directors:
Bruce Page, E F. Peacock,

139 Elm Park Mansions
Park Walk
London, S.W.10.

Mr David Caute,
The New Statesman,
10 Great Turnstile,
London, W.C.1.

30th October 1979.

Dear Caute,

    Thank you for your roneod reply to my letter of 23rd October,
applying for the post of Assistant Literary Editor under you.

    'I apologise for sending you a standard reply', you wrote.

    Your apologies are not accepted. I thought you left-wingers
were all for brotherly love and the small man (not that I'm a small
man, you understand. Merely a novice in the world of letters.)

    In applying for the job I took the trouble of sending examples
of my work in progress, to show I was qualified for the job. The
least you could have done was cast your eye over these and append
your valuable assessment. Raymond Mortimer must be turning in his
grave at such high-handedness from one of his successors.

    I now return my work in progress and look forward to receiving
your comments.

    Yours sincerely,

Henry Root.

PS. Sorry to see Julian Barnes is back. I thought you'd got rid
of him. Why don't you employ a TV critic with something to say like
Richard Ingrams?

Copy to Bruce Page.

Dear Mr Root,
    Your stuff has no interest for me.
Anything further from you will go into the
wastepaper basket.
    David Caute

139 Elm Park Mansions
Park Walk
London, S.W.10.

Mrs Mary Whitehouse,
National Viewers and Listeners Association,
Ardleigh,
Colchester,
Essex.   24th October 1979.

Dear Mrs Whitehouse,

So! According to your doctor you've lost your voice because
you talk too much.

This blow comes at a time when we can ill afford your vocal
absence from the 'media' scene. Who else is to speak out against
the pornographers, left-wing subversives and gay Christians coming
out of the toilet? Wherever one looks, the family is being threatened.

Couldn't we get a second opinion?

Please God your voice will soon return. Meanwhile here's an
amusing anecdote which may help to cheer you up. Miss Sally Ann
Voak, 'The Sun's' expert on health, diet, yoga, astrology, levitation,
foreplay, transcendental meditation and related difficulties wrote
an article recently explaining how top Hollywood lovelies live longer
and lead an active sex life well into old age ('Ginger Rogers! And
She's 76!') by observing strict eating habits. In the course of her
reseraches for the article, Miss Voak spoke to several top Hollywood
lovelies on the telephone, including Telly Savalas (TV's Kojak!) He
admitted that he often forgot his diet, stuffing himself instead with
unhealthy junk foods.

"I have this problem," he growled. "I've got this sweet tooth.
I can't resist ice-cream with lashings of chocolate sauce."

"Crushed nuts?" asked Sally.

"No," said Telly. "Just a touch of laryngitis."

Eh? Not bad? It helps to have a good laugh, don't you think?

How about a signed photo, Mary? If you're to be 'off the scene'
for a while, it would be nice to have a really good picture to
remember you by. Being a retiring sort of person, only allowing
yourself to be dragged into the limelight by your sense of duty to
the community, you may not keep a stack of photos handy, but I'm
sure you must have an old snap-shot somewhere you could let me have.
I enclose a pound to cover your expenses.

Get well soon!

Yours sincerely,

Henry Root.

Henry Root.

NATIONAL VIEWERS' AND LISTENERS' ASSOCIATION

Hon. General Secretary :
Mrs. MARY WHITEHOUSE
Ardleigh, Colchester
Essex CO7 7RH

Tel. Colchester 230123

26th October 1979

Mr. Henry Root,
139 Elm Park Mansions,
Park Walk,
London SW10.

Dear Mr. Root,

Thank you very much for your very kind letter to Mrs. Whitehouse and most generous contribution towards expenses.

I'm afraid she really does have to cut down the amount of public speaking she undertakes, but as requested I have pleasure in enclosing a photograph.

Yours sincerely,

Mrs. A. Boyle
Secretary to Mrs. Whitehouse

139 Elm Park Mansions
Park Walk
London, S.W.10.

P.C. Jim Jardine,
The Police Federation,
15-17 Langley Road,
Surbiton,
Surrey KT6 6LP.   26th October 1979.

Dear Constable Jardine,

Your recent letter in 'The Guardian' (my chauffeur takes it),
in which you pointed out that the unfortunate murder of Blair Peach
was retaliation by the Police for the killing of P.C. Kellam, had
my whole-hearted support. As you said, this made the score, in a
sense, one all.

However, a recent letter in 'The New Statesman' (my daughter
Doreen (20) takes it) from Mr Michael Meacher MP suggests that the
Police are in fact winning this particular contest, and by a
commendably wide margin. Mr Meacher pointed out that between 1970
and 1976 45 people died from non-natural causes while helping the
police with their enquiries, excluding suicide.

Even with the recent murder of a detective in Gloucester, that
makes the score:

The Police 46 - The General Public 2.

Not bad, and a clear refutation of the view being put about
that the police are losing the fight against lawlessness. Well done!

While I have your attention, might I point out that you never
answered my letter of 23rd April 1979, in which I asked you whether
my local candidate at the General Election, Mr Nicholas Scott, was
an officially approved Law and Order Candidate, supported by the
Police Federation.

I would have thought that law and order started with answering
letters!

Let's hope you answer this one!

Yours sincerely,

Henry Root

Henry Root.

Police Federation OF ENGLAND AND WALES

15·17 Langley Road Surbiton Surrey KT6 6LP Tel: 01·399 2224 (4 Lines)

Established by Act of Parliament

Our Ref: JTJ/MF

Your Ref:

31st October, 1979

Mr.Henry Root,
139, Elm Park Mansions,
Park Walk,
London, S.W.10.

Dear Mr.Root,

The short answer to your letters of 23rd April and 26th October 1979 is that I am far too busy with matters of real importance to bandy words with you on facetious comments. I note, however, that you choose to ignore the murder of five police officers in the period 1970-1976, which is a good indication of your general attitude.

On points of fact; I never said that the death of Blair Peach could be regarded as police retaliation for the murder of P.C.Kellam. As Mr.Peach died in April and Mr.Kellam in October, you will see that you were talking nonsense in attributing such a statement to me.

Two, there has been no 'recent murder of a detective in Gloucester'.

Three, the Police Federation does not, and never has, supported a political party or candidate. At the General Election we wrote to every candidate setting out our views on the question of the rule of law.

I am sorry to have to spoil your fantasies with facts.

Yours sincerely,

J.T.JARDINE
Chairman

Please reply to the Secretary

139 Elm Park Mansions
Park Walk
London, S.W.10.

P.C. Jim Jardine,
The Police Federation,
15-17 Langley Road,
Surbiton,
Surrey.   3rd November 1979.

Dear Constable,

I have before me your discourteous letter of 31st October in
reply to mine of 26th October.

If this is the manner in which you write to those who support
the work the police do, how on earth do you write to those who, in
the words of that fine man, Mr James Anderton, are engaged in an
orchestrated attempt to bring the police (and therefore democracy
itself) into disrepute?

Goats and monkeys, man, I'm on your side! I was merely congratulating you for having the courage in these sentimental times
to draw the public's attention to the fact that the Police do a very
dangerous job which they can only prosecute effectively by occasionally
resorting to over-robust methods. What's controversial about that?

I'm sorry I got the score wrong and I'm grateful to you for
pointing out that it should read:

The Police 46 - The General Public 7.

Thank you for correcting the two other errors in my letter.
I am of course delighted that there has been no recent murder of
a detective in Gloucester. And I quite see that you couldn't have
said that the Blair Peach murder was in retaliation for the murder
of P.C. Kellam. I must have misread your letter in 'The Guardian'.
Perhaps you could let me know whose murder it was that triggered off
the Blair Peach killing?

I look forward to hearing from you.

Yours sincerely,

Henry Root.

Henry Root.
Copy to Sir David McNee.

Police Federation OF ENGLAND AND WALES

15·17 Langley Road Surbiton Surrey KT6 6LP Tel: 01·399 2224 (4 Lines)

Established by Act of Parliament

Our Ref: JTJ/MF

9th November, 1979

Your Ref:

Mr.H.Root,
139, Elm Park Mansions,
Park Walk,
London, S.W.10.

Dear Mr.Root,

    I have read again your original letter, in the light of your second one. I may well have mistaken your ironical style and misjudged your intentions, in which case I am quite happy to apologise.

    Let me make it clear, however, that I am not going to accept all the premises in your letters. I must reject the idea that there is a 'score' to be kept; those "killed by the police" and "police killed by the public". In the latter, there is no doubt of the cause of death. In the former, except for a number of cases where police officers have been forced to shoot armed criminals or deranged persons who were threatening others with firearms, the cause of death is inconclusive. Mr.Meacher's references to 42 people who have died in police custody from other than natural causes or suicide is gravely misleading. Inquests are held in such circumstances and my information suggests that in only two cases in recent years have inquests recorded verdicts which blame the police for the deaths.

    Nor do I accept that people have been killed by the police in acts of vengeance. I must repeat, I have never suggested that the death of Blair Peach was in retaliation for the death of any police officer. All that I said was that people who raised an outcry over his death remained silent when a police officer was killed. The Police Federation would never support a criminal action by a police officer. We are not in the business of revenge. Our concern is with the maintenance of the rule of law and the certainty of justice.

    If my first reply was couched in rather peremptory terms, I should explain that I received a large number of 'pro' and 'anti' letters about the Peach case. Some of the 'anti' letters made the point about deaths in police custody, so I may have formed a wrong idea of your point of view.

                Yours sincerely,

                J.T.JARDINE
                Chairman

Please reply to the Secretary

139 Elm Park Mansions
Park Walk
London, S.W.I0.

Mr Michael Parkinson,
The BBC,
Television Centre,
London, W.I2.
26th October 1979.

Dear Michael,

Following the great success of 'David Jacobs's Book of
Celebrities' Jokes and Anecdotes', I have been commissioned by
Robson Books to produce 'The Celebrities' Book of Embarrassing
Incidents!'.

In compiling a draft list of humiliating incidents showing
that celebrities are human like the rest of us but more so, I have
discovered that many of the most hilarious anecdotes were first
aired publicly on your lively 'chat' show. I have therefore
managed to persuade Robson Books to let me rope you in as co-Editor
on the grounds that having your name on the writing-paper will
make it easier for us to collect a fund of good stories from well-
known 'personalities'.

I hope you'll agree with this arrangement. The concept
strikes me as very solid - not least because the 'celebrities' will
do all the work! All we'll have to do is listen to their anecdotes.
And we won't have to pay them much, if anything! A fiver an
anecdote should keep them quiet and we can cop all the royalties!

Since the concept's mine, I suggest that you and I split
the take 70/30 in my favour. Let me know if this suits you and
I'll instruct Robsons to draw up the contracts.

I look forward to hearing from you. We could make a lot of
easy money on this one, Michael!

Keep pitching 'em on middle-and-leg!

Yours sincerely,

Henry Root

Henry Root.

139 Elm Park Mansions
Park Walk
London, S.W.10.

The Commanding Officer,
The Royal Marines School of Music,
Deal,
Kent.   29th October 1979.

Dear General,

    I should like to enlist my boy Henry Jr under your firm
command as soon as possible.

    The lad's just turned 16 and frankly he's in shocking shape.
He sits around in his room all day, trying on his sister's clothes,
painting his finger nails and dreaming of life as a rock and roll
crooner.

    Short of sending him to one of Mr Willie Whitehouse's 'short,
sharp shock detention camps' (I've applied for a place at one of these,
but have so far received no reply from Mr Whitehouse) I see nothing
for it but a career in the services on the musical side of things.

    I gather he plays the trumpet, though his repertoire at the
moment is restricted to a version of Miss Channing Pollock's hit
tune 'Hullo Dolly'. I suppose that's a start.

    It so happens that I have just joined the Royal Cinq Ports
Golf Club at Deal and will be driving down with Mrs Root to inspect
the links on Sunday November 11th, so if it will be convenient for
you, Mrs Root and I will drop in on you in the afternoon of that
day to discuss the arrangements.

    I gather that 'a bit goes on' after lights-out in a military
atmosphere and (since Henry Jr needs little encouragement in this
area in my judgement) I wonder whether he could have a private room?
I'm told that you don't have to get up very early in the morning
to catch the Royal Marines with their trousers down these days.
Sign of the times.

    I look forward to hearing from you, General.

    Tell it to the Marines! Let's go!

    Yours sincerely,

    Henry Root

    Henry Root.

139 Elm Park Mansions
Park Walk
London, S.W.10.

The Commanding Officer,
The Royal Marines,
State House,
High Holborn,   11th November 1979.
London, W.C.1.

Dear General,

My boy Henry Jr wears tights and plays the trumpet so, calcu-
lating that a career in the Marines might straighten him out, I wrote
to the Commanding Officer of the Royal Marines School of Music on
29th October, saying that Mrs Root and I would drop in on him on Sunday
11th November to chat things over.

Receiving no reply, I sent him a telegram a few days later asking
him whether he was expecting us. To my amazement I received no reply
to this either!

What's going on? Aren't you keen to recruit? I'd be most
grateful, General, if you'd look into this on my behalf, signalling
a rocket, if you deem it appropriate, to your fellow at Deal.

Support the Iron Lady!

Yours sincerely,

Henry Root

Henry Root.

**Royal Navy, Royal Marines and
Women's Royal Naval Service**
State House High Holborn London WC1R 4TG

Telephone 01-405 9951 ext 53

	Your reference	
H Root Esq		
139 Elm Park Mansions	Our reference	LON 713/2
Park Walk		
London SW10	Date	13 November 1979

Dear Mr Root,

Thank you for your letter dated 11 November 1979.

I well appreciate the concern you must feel regarding your son, and his ambition to join the Royal Marines as a Musician.

At this stage I have no idea why your letter and telegram to the Commanding Officer RM School of Music were unanswered, but I can say that your letter to me, will be forwarded through the appropriate channels.

If Henry would make a formal application to the Careers Information Office State House (Reply card enclosed) then we will be delighted to see him, and I wish him luck in his application.

I am sorry that you have been caused any inconvenience, and hope that Henry will achieve his ambition.

Yours sincerely

Andrew Reive

Royal Marines School of Music
Deal
Kent
Deal 62121 **Ext** 296

SM 20/12/1

Mr H ROOT
139 Elm Park Mansions
Park Walk   **29**   Nov 79
London SW10

CAREER COUNSELLING

Reference:

A. Letter dated 29 Oct 79

1. Thank you for the letter concerning possible enlistment for your son, Reference A.

2. It is requested that all detail be passed to:

Department of Naval Recruiting
Ministry of Defence
Old Admiralty Building
Spring Gardens
London SW1A 2BE.

S DOWN
Capt RM
        RMSM

139 Elm Park Mansions
Park Walk
London, S.W.10.

Mr Michael Ivens,
40 Doughty Street,
London, W.C.1.   5th November 1979.

Dear Mr Ivens,

        You will have been as shocked as I was to discover that in
spite of two humiliating defeats in the courts, the vendetta conducted
by 'Private Eye' against Sir James Goldsmith continues apace.

        As you will have seen, an appeal to finance further cowardly
assaults has just been set up by 'Private Eye' under the lamentably
crude title of The Gillardballs Fund, but after four weeks of dis-
traught pleading they have only been able to raise the paltry sum
of £515.50.

        To counter this, I and a few of Sir James's closest associates
have formed 'The Friends of Sir James Goldsmith Against Moles in the
Media Fund'. Various money-raising activities are planned and you may
wish to show your solidity by joining a counter-revolutionary march
which Paul Johnson has organised for Sunday 25th November.

        Capitalists will muster at noon outside the Bank of England to
participate in a programme of traditional right-wing, two-nations
activities, the funds from which will go to the Sir James Goldsmith
Appeal. Carrying banners proclaiming such divisive Tory messages as
'Greed is a Moral Responsibility!', 'Freedom to Rob under the Law!',
'Asset-Strippers Lib!', 'Support the Opaque Society!', "Winning is
Good Business!' and 'It's All About Profits!', we will march first
to Transport House, where we will burn stuffed effigies of Lenin,
Benn, Vanessa Redgrave and Moss Hart on the steps outside and then
make our presence known through the letter-box.

        To demonstrate that elitism has an acceptable face, we shall
then distribute food hampers from Fortnums among the low-paid workers
of St George's Hospital before taking a party of miners' kiddies on
a conducted tour of Westminster School (by arrangement with my friend
Sir John Rae) so that they will discover the advantages they are
missing because of their parents' lamentable lack of drive and prudence. First they will be confused by having Latin insults bellowed
at them by the scholars of the sixth form; then they will be debagged
and tossed into the Thames by the rowing eight; finally they will be
flogged off the premises with damp towels and sent home whimpering
to their parents.

        Tired but satisfied, we will then respond to the Chelsea area,
sneering at liberals, social security scroungers, boat-persons and
kid-glove pansies on the way. Here we'll duff up a couple of lame
ducks outside Sir Keith Joseph's delightful house in Mulberry Walk,

where sherry wine will be purveyed in his charming lounge-room
prior to an address on the virtues of monetarism.

I know Johnson will be most upset if you can't make it, and
Sir James himself, needless to say, would take a very dim view of
your failure to attend!

I look forward to hearing from you.

Yours sincerely,

Henry Root.

139 Elm Park Mansions
Park Walk
London, S.W.10.

The Commissioner,
The City of London Police,
26 Old Jewry,   5th November 1979.
London, E.C.2.

Dear Commissioner,

    I enclose a copy of a letter which is being sent out to various leading capitalists concerning a monetarist demonstration planned for Sunday 25th November.

    Since the march sets forth from a spot on your territory, I imagine that your permission for assemble might be necessary.

    I take it that this will be immediately forthcoming since it is hardly to be conceived that a group of City gentlemen will comport themselves except with due regard for the requirements of law and order. Banners will be carried, but chanting will be kept to a minimum.

    I look forward to hearing from you with the necessary permissions, and I would like to say that you would be more than welcome on the march yourself, albeit you're only a policeman. I imagine that you will be sympathetic with its aims.

    Yours sincerely,

Henry Root

Henry Root.

TELEPHONE 01-606 8866
EXT 226
TELEGRAMS ADJUTOR LONDON TELEX

OFFICIAL LETTERS TO BE ADDRESSED
THE COMMISSIONER OF POLICE
FOR THE CITY OF LONDON

PLEASE QUOTE REF   M2/1617/79
YOUR REF

CITY OF LONDON POLICE
"A" Department
37 Wood Street
London EC2V 7HN

Dear Mr. Root,   8th November, 1979

    I am directed by the Commissioner of Police for the City of London to acknowledge your letter of the 5th November, 1979, referring to a proposed demonstration on Sunday, 25th November, 1979.

    In order to discuss your proposals and arrange police coverage for the event I should be grateful if you would telephone this office so that an appointment can be made.

    Yours sincerely,

Chief Superintendent

Mr. H. Root,
139, Elm Park Mansions,
Park Walk,
London, S.W.10.

 THE FREE ENTERPRISE ORGANISATION

Henry Root Esq   14th November 1979
139 Elm Park Mansions
Park Walk
<u>LONDON S W 1O</u>

Dear Mr (....) Root

     Many thanks for your kind invitation to march.
But I am afraid I must decline to walk behind deathbed
converts. Moreover, Private Eye is the only paper
that has ever carried the word "nice" about me, even
though it was quoted from somebody.

     My regards to Mrs Root, whom I seem to remember
once having met under curious circumstances in the
Levant.

                         Yours

                         Michael Ivens

40 Doughty Street, London WC1N 2LF   Tel: 01-405 5195

139 Elm Park Mansions
Park Walk
London, S.W.10.

The General Secretary,
The National Union of Journalists,
Acorn House,
314 Gray's Inn Road,
London, W.C.1.

5th November 1979.

Sir,
    I wish to complain about the behaviour of one of your members,
Mr Geoffrey Wheatcroft.

    I am presently engaged on the compilation of an Anthology of
Great Modern British Prose, and I wrote to him on 23rd August seeking
his permission to incorporate passages by himself, Mr Richard Ingrams,
Mr Taki, Mr George Gale and Dr Patrick Cosgrave, all of which first
appeared in 'The Spectator', of which periodical Mr Wheatcroft is,
as you may know, temporarily the Literary Editor.

    Receiving no reply, I wrote to him again on 15th September.
To this letter I got a note from his 'personal' secretary, Miss
Clare Asquith, apologising for Wheatcroft's general slackness and
high-handedness (part and parcel of being well-born and working
for a Tory magazine, no doubt) and saying that she'd be only too
happy to put a squib up him.

    Since I heard nothing further, I wrote again on 21st October,
asking what was going on. To my utter amazement, I have received
no reply to this letter at all!

    What can you do? Can you drum him out of the union, so that
he is no longer in a position (arrived at, no doubt, by the in-born
ability to skip with the agility of a mountain goat up the sturdy
mesh of the old-boy network) to obstruct the serious work of those
with a less dilettante attitude to the world of letters?

    I look forward to hearing from you.

Yours sincerely,

Henry Root

Henry Root.

Copy to Geoffrey Wheatcroft.

NATIONAL UNION OF JOURNALISTS

Acorn House, 314/320 Gray's Inn Road, London WC1X 8DP
Telephone: 01-278 7916

Dictated 10th December 1979

c.c. General Secretary

CCM/G

12th December 1979,

Mr. Henry Root,
139 Elm Park Mansions,
Park Walk,
London S.W.10.

Dear Mr. Root,

Thank you for your letter to the General Secretary of November 5th. I must apologise for the delay in replying but I took my annual holiday in a lump this year and it has taken some time to catch up on back correspondence which had been passed over to me to handle.

Frankly I do not think there is anything that I can do to help you over your problem about getting Mr. Wheatcroft to give his permission to use passages by himself in your anthology of Great Modern British Prose. I am surprised that he is reluctant to give you permission unless he thinks that his work only qualifies for an anthology of Superb Modern British Prose, but his actions are not really ones that fall within the general requirements of the Union's Code of Conduct.

The only action the Union could take is if another Union member laid a complaint against Mr. Wheatcroft that he was guilty of a breach of our Code of Conduct, but I am afraid the behaviour about which you complain does not really fall within the terms of that Code of Conduct.

The only practical suggestion that I can offer is that you might perhaps write a tongue-in-cheek letter for publication in the Spectator saying that you are writing an anthology of Great Modern British Prose and you are somewhat staggered at the modesty of some people who are unwilling to give permission to have their prose appear in such an anthology.

Such reluctance perhaps maybe attributed to excessive modesty or an incredible lack of self-confidence in the prose itself.

A letter along those lines appearing in the Spectator might perhaps flush Mr. Wheatcroft out, I don't know?

The other flash of inspiration which has just occurred to me is that if the prose appeared in the Spectator the copyright therefore may belong really to the magazine itself since Mr. Wheatcroft as an employee gives up that copyright to the publication which employs him. You could therefore perhaps write to the Editor of the Spectator and seek his permission as Editor to reproduce work that has appeared in the magazine. Beyond that all I can suggest is that the preface to the anthology might say that work by certain people would have appeared but for their failure to give permission for it to appear. It is not unknown for prefaces to both thank people for their help and sometimes not thank people for their lack of help!

Yours sincerely,

CHARLES HARKNESS, DEPUTY GENERAL SECRETARY

139 Elm Park Mansions
Park Walk
London, S.W.10.

Mr Malcolm Muggeridge,
c/o The BBC,
Television Centre,
London, W.12.   5th November 1979.

Dear Mr Muggeridge,
     I am naturally most disappointed not to have received the
courtesy of a reply to my letter of 4th October, particularly
since I enclosed the postage.
     I suppose you want money too for the cost of the photo. Sorry!
I should have thought of that. I now enclose a pound, which I
trust covers your expenses adequately in the matter.
     I look forward to hearing from you.
     Yours sincerely,

     Henry Root.

     Henry Root.

          This letter is extremely insolent. I have been
     abroad and only lately returned, and have no trace
     of your previous letter in a large accumulation of
     mail.

Mr Malcolm Muggeridge,
c/o The BBC,
Television Centre,
London, W.12.

139 Elm Park Mansions
Park Walk
London, S.W.10.

10th November 1979.

Dear Mr Muggeridge,

Congratulations on your recent performance on the TV Show, 'Friday, Saturday Morning'!

Your massive intellect soon reduced those so-called zany young men from Monty Python to quivering jelly and your awesome moral authority threw a cruel spotlight on their cheap, blasphemous jests. Well done! I found your performance inspirational, but my daughter Doreen, with whom I was watching, had her usual silly quibbles.

At one point you averred that you had once asked Sister Teresa what was the difference between her and a social worker. She had replied, you said, that a social worker was inspired by an idea, whereas she was inspired by Christ. Were Christ to be revealed as not being who he claimed to be, she said, her work would be over. To which my daughter Doreen exclaimed:

"How disgraceful! If that is truly Sister Teresa's position, then her work has no ethical foundation whatsoever. If she does good work merely because she imagines herself to be commanded to do so by Christ, her position is morally symmetrical to that of a person who does evil work because he imagines himself charged to do so by the Devil. Albeit her work has good consequences, no more credit should be given to her than blame should attach to the man who is commanded by the Devil. If her explanation is that she recognises Christ's teachings as good, then, like the social worker, she is inspired by an idea. If she doesn't recognise Christ's teachings as good (by some other yardstick) why does she follow them? Either Sister Teresa's position is incoherent or, which is more likely, Muggeridge's account of it is."

Well, that's all gibberish to me, Malcolm, but I would be very grateful if you could explain the fallacy in her argument so that I can confound the irreverend young chit.

Later she took exception to your saying that were a blashemous film to be made about Mohammad 'all the anti-racialists would be up in arms'. "Is not Muggeridge an anti-racialist?" she asked. So what if you're not!

Sorry you haven't replied yet to my letter of 4th October, nor to the follow-up with which I enclosed a pound. Don't worry. I expect you're a very busy man. Incidentally, ignore the PS to my first letter. It seems that the lady I mistook for your wife was in fact Mr Quentin Crisp, the male model. Sorry!

Yours sincerely,

Henry Root

Henry Root.

139 Elm Park Mansions
Park Walk
London, S.W.10.

22nd November 1979.

Mr Malcolm Muggeridge,
The BBC,
Television Centre,
London, W.12.

Dear Mr Muggeridge,

Frankly I'm baffled. On 5th November I wrote to you in the most civil terms, enquiring as to whether you had yet had time to digest the contents of, and formulate a reply to, an earlier and equally civil letter. To boot, I enclosed a pound to cover your expenses in the matter.

To my astonishment you returned my letter of 5th November, on which you had appendixed an unsigned note to the effect that it was extremely insolent!

In what consists the insolence? I do not accept your thinking on this, and now return the pound, pending an explanation.

All I want is a photograph of yourself (pulling, if possible, one of your funny faces) to add to Mrs Root's collection of media celebrities. What's wrong with that? You are reacting, if I may say so, like some immature crooner or association football player bleating about the invasion of his privacy consequent upon his becoming a 'personality'. If you don't like the heat in the kitchen I suggest you repair forthwith to the loungeroom. You should have thought of the pressures at the top before aiming yourself thither with such singleness of purpose.

Let's have a little Christian humility, Malcolm!

Yours sincerely,

Henry Root

Henry Root.

139 Elm Park Mansions
Park Walk
London, S.W.10.

Professor Sir A.J. Ayer,
10 Regents Park Terrace,
London, N.W.1.

17th November 1979.

Dear Sir Alfred,

I'm told you're qualified to settle two disputes - on the subjects of football and philosophy - currently raging in my loungeroom.

1. Last night the BBC News featured a football match between Ipswich and England.

"This isn't a game of football," expostulated my daughter Doreen (20), "it's a category mistake."

What was she talking about? It looked like a game of football to me.

B. Last weekend we were watching the TV show 'Friday Night, Saturday Morning', in which that eminent thinker Mr Malcolm Muggeridge was putting two zany young upstarts from 'Monty Python' through the threshing machine of his massive intellect. Discussing blasphemy, Muggeridge observed that he had once asked that saintly woman Mother Teresa to define the difference between herself and a mere social worker. She had replied that a social worker was inspired by nothing more than an idea, whereas she was inspired by a person, namely Christ. Were Christ to be revealed as not being who he claimed to be, she has said to Muggeridge, her work would be over. She would have no further interest in doing good. At this point my daughter Doreen declaimed:

"If that is a true account of Mother Teresa's position, her work has no ethical foundation at all. If she does good work merely because she imagines herself to be commanded to do so by Christ, her position is morally symmetrical to that of a person who does evil work because he imagines himself to be commanded to do so by the devil. Albeit her work is good, no more credit should accrue to her than blame to the man who is commanded by the devil. If her explanation is that she recognises Christ's teachings as good, then, like the social worker, she _is_ inspired by an idea. If she doesn't recognise them as good (by some independent criterion) why does she follow them? Either her position, or Muggeridge's account of it, is utterly incoherent. I suspect the latter. Poor old fool".

I'm sure my Doreen's talking nonsense and I think it important in the interests of law and order that the young chit be confounded. Could you pronounce her mistaken in a few crisp, well-chosen sentences? I'd be obliged.

Yours sincerely,

Henry Root

Henry Root.

10 REGENTS PARK TERRACE

LONDON NWI 7EE

01-485 4855

28 November 1979.

Dear Mr. Root:

The term "category mistake" was introduced
into philosophy by my old tutor, Gilbert Ryle.
You will find that he makes considerable use of
it in his famous book, <u>The Concept of Mind</u>.
The point of your daughter's joke was presumably
that since the England team is a national football
side and Ipswich Town only a club side, they
belong to different categories.

On your second point your daughter is simply
right.   Many philosophers, including Leibniz and
Russell, have pointed out that morals cannot be
founded on authority.

Yours sincerely,

A. J A

Professor Sir Alfred Ayer.

139 Elm Park Mansions
Park Walk
London, S.W.10.

Gay Noel Music Ltd,   21st November 1979.
24 Denmark Street,
London, W.C.2.

Dear gay Noel,

Having occasion just now to look up the telephone number of
Gay Nites Women's Lingerie (Mrs Root's birthday looming, alas!) my
eye caught your entry in the directory - Gay Noel Music Co Ltd.

Well done! I admire a man who admits of his proclivities publicly, and what could be more public than the telephone directory?
It so happens that you might be in a position to help me. It is
becoming increasingly obvious to me that my boy Henry Jr (15), insofar as he wears tights and paints his fingernails, is of your
stripe. Nothing wrong with that. The fact is too that the lad
plays the guitar and pens songs of a protest nature, so I'm won-
dering whether you'd like to take him on?

Of course you'll want to see the lad and hear his stuff before
committing yourself to representation, so I'll bring him in plus
tapes at 3pm next Tuesday week, 4th December. Let me know if this
won't suit. I'd hate to run through the door of your office to
find you were being attended to by your masseur in another part.

I look forward to meeting you on the 4th!

Yours sincerely,

Henry Root

Henry Root.

THE RICHARD ARMITAGE—NOEL GAY ORGANISATION LTD

NOEL GAY ARTISTS LIMITED

Registered Office: 24 DENMARK STREET . LONDON . WC2H 8NJ
Telephone: 01-836 3941/5 · 01-240 0451/4
Grams: Noelgay London WC2H 8NJ · Cables: Noelgay London Telex · Telex No: 21760

30th November, 1979

Henry Root, Esq.,
139 Elm Park Mansions,
Park Walk,
LONDON. SW10.

Dear Mr. Root,

Your letter dated November 21st.

I am afraid the Company can in no circumstances audition composers
in the first instance. Should you wish to send tapes they will be carefully
listened to.

Yours sincerely,

Lorraine Hamilton

Directors: R N M Armitage . R C Walker . G X Constantinidi . R Germains
Licensed in accordance with the Employment Agencies Act 1973-No. SE(A) 612
Members of the Agents Association Ltd. Registered in England No. 610415
An offer in this letter does not constitute a contract

139 Elm Park Mansions
Park Walk
London, S.W.10.

Michael Rubinstein Esq,
6 Raymond Buildings,
Grays Inn,
London, W.C.1.   3rd December 1979.

Dear Mr Rubinstein,

I'm told you know a certain amount of law, being commendably
quick to act against those who commit a slur or slander.

Well done!

I'd like you to represent me in a matter of some delicacy but
with a high profit potential. From the enclosed correspondence, you
will immediately see that I had occasion some weeks ago to to invite
certain well-positioned folk to join a monetarist march, organised
by my friend Paul Johnson. One such receiving an invitation was
Mr Michael Ivens of the Free Enterprise Organisation, AIMS.

Imagine my surprise when I received his reply, a copy of which
I now enclose! I have quizzed Mrs Root most vigorously re the thrust
of his accusation and I am satisfied that she has never been near
the Levant (indeed she has never even heard of it) and that she has
never met Mr Ivens under curious or any other circumstances.

This being so, you will agree with me, I take it, that Mr
Ivens's letter constitutes a libel of a most disagreeable kind and
insofar as my 'personal' secretary has read it, damage has already
been caused, with many jokes of an off-colour nature being promul-
gated in the typing-pool.

I imagine that upon institution of proceedings recompense
of an unusually punitive weight would be awarded to me in the High
Court, and since I am eager to get this action under way as soon as
possible, I would welcome the opportunity of an early conference.

Might I, incidentally, congratulate you on the way you have
handled yourself in your many media appearances re the recent 'Professor' Blunt revelations? Being a plain man who has worked his way
to the top of the pile in wet fish by the sweat of his brow and of
those under him, I have little time for antique dealers, art histor-
ians of a Neopolitan bent, thirties pansies and full Colonels in
the KGB who infiltrate her Majesty's household. But you were only
doing your job. Nothing wrong with that.

I look forward to your providing me with the same excellent
service.

Let's make money here!

Yours sincerely,

Henry Root

Henry Root.

MICHAEL RUBINSTEIN   A. J. HUCKER   JOAN RUBINSTEIN   ANTHONY RUBINSTEIN
M. C. FOWLER   RICHARD N. SAX   T. K. H. ROBERTSON   M. ALEXANDER
R. I. YONGE   THOMAS HALL   MARGARET A. BROWN
CONSULTANT: P. A. H. CLARK

6, RAYMOND BUILDINGS,
GRAYS INN, LONDON, WCIR 5BZ.
TELEGRAMS: RUBINSTEIN LONDON W C I
TELEX NO. 21143 WNANDW G
TELEPHONE: 01-242 8404

7th December, 1979

YOUR REF

OUR REF MR/AS

Henry Root, Esq.,
139 Elm Park Mansions,
Park Walk,
London, S.W.10.

Dear Mr. Root,

Thank you for your letter of the 3rd December. I very much appreciate your kind remarks about my handling of the "'Professor' Blunt revelations". (There is no need to put 'Professor' into quotation marks since he still has the right to be called by that title.)

Mr. Michael Ivens' letter does not appear to be headed "Confidential" but I gather that it was addressed only to you, presumably on the envelope as well as on the letter itself. The mysterious reference to your wife in the second paragraph if it were deemed defamatory of her, which is by no means certain, might entitle her to claim damages for libel in view of the publication of the letter to a third party, namely yourself, but would not, on the face of it, entitle you to succeed in such a claim. That your 'personal' secretary has seen Mr. Ivens' letter and as a result jokes, holding you or your wife up to ridicule, may be told in the typing-pool causing you damage, as you say, will not necessarily affect the interests of Mrs. Root in any possible claim against Mr. Ivens nor, of itself, entitle <u>you</u> to make such a claim.

The first question, therefore, is whether your wife would wish to make a claim against Mr. Ivens in respect of what you and perhaps she believed to be a defamatory innuendo in the last paragraph of his letter of the 14th November, which she would have to claim libels her to you and probably to you alone. I do not know myself whether the reference to a meeting "under curious circumstances in the Levant" would be recognised by anyone as necessarily involving a defamatory innuendo. This might be possible or it might be hard to prove. I think it more likely, however, that it would be defensible by Mr. Ivens if he chose to defend any claim made against him, as would be almost certain, as only intended as a harmless joke in the context of a friendly reply to your letter to him of the 9th November which, I am bound to say, reads to me as deliberately light-hearted although I appreciate that you may have intended it as politically serious. If I am right about the way that a jury would be inclined or persuaded to interpret this exchange of correspondence then I must tell you (and Mrs. Root through you) that there would be no prospect at all of either of you making money out of a claim against Mr. Ivens. You would have to place a substantial sum at stake before deciding to initiate proceedings and a sum well into five figures might be at risk should the action proceed to trial - in some two or three years time. Meanwhile, I am sure you would find that any possible damage done to either of you in the typing-pool would have been dissipated by the normal respect expected of those who work there and you might well recognise the disadvantages to you both of the prospect of being made to look ridiculous for having brought the action if the Plaintiff were to lose it or to be awarded only nominal or contemptuous damages at the end of the day.

You will understand from what I have written above that my advice is to ignore Mr. Ivens' letter and to put the whole incident behind you - and Mrs. Root too, of course.

If you are dissatisfied with the above advice then I shall be glad to see you by appointment and would ask you to let me have a sum of £50.00 on account for costs incurred and to be incurred. Should you decide to take the matter no further, in accordance with my advice, I would appreciate your notifying me of that decision and would then propose to make no charge whatsoever for my advice in this letter.

Yours sincerely,

139 Elm Park Mansions
Park Walk
London, S.W.10.

Ms Jean Rook,
The Daily Express,
Fleet Street,   5th December 1979.
London, E.C.4.

Dear Jean,

    So - they call you the biggest bitch in Fleet Street! Nothing
wrong with that. Well done!

    I have read your column with interest for many years. You seem
like a sensible old trout and you write with unusual flair. More to
the point, you always take a healthily pragmatic attitude to life's
many problems, and that is why I now address you.

    Frankly, Jean, I have for some time been casting round for an
excuse to dump Mrs Root. She's been a good mother to my two children,
Doreen (20) and Henry Jr (15), but she doesn't shape up too well on
all occasions and since, after many years of striving, I am at long
last getting somewhere in cafe society I would welcome upon my arm on
occasions involving the boulevardier Norman St John Stevas and others
of that ilk a somewhat younger woman.

    It so happens that the opportunity I've been waiting for seems
to have come my way. I have just received an extraordinary letter
from Mr Michael Ivens of the Free Enterprise Organisation, AIMS, in
which he alleges that he was familiar with Mrs Root 'under curious
circumstances in the Levant'.

    Whether this allegation is true or not, it seems that I have
two possible courses of action open to me. I can either line my
pocket by bringing (via Rubinstein) an action for libel against this
fellow Ivens (by no means a man of straw from all I hear), or I can
take this opportunity of showing Mrs Root the door on the grounds
that she has cuckolded me with the aforesaid Ivens.

    Which should I do, Jean? To assist you in framing your advice,
I enclose a typical picture of Mrs Root. It was taken on an occasion
when, unmindful of the fact that we had guests of some consequence
in our loungeroom, she suddenly removed her clothes, put some Russiam
music on the gramaphone and danced the mazurka with a rabbit on her
head. Albeit we're a musical household (it is not unusual for us
after dinner to entertain our guests with the cast album of 'Oliver'
or 'Hullo Dolly') this was going too far.

    I realise that you don't purport to be a kind of thinking man's
Anna Raeburn, so I enclose a stamped addressed envelope for the
courtesy of your advice in the matter and for the safe return of
the snap of Mrs Root, which Rubinstein will no doubt need as evidence in such proceedings as I may decide to bring.

    I look forward to hearing from you, Jean!

    Yours,

    Henry Root
    Henry Root.

DAILY EXPRESS

Express
Newspapers
Limited

121 Fleet Street
London EC4P 4JT
Telephone
01-353 8000
Telex No 21841
Cable Address
Express London

11 December 1979

Mr H Root
139 Elm Park Mansions
Park Walk
LONDON
SW10

Dear Mr Root

Thank you for your letter.

I am certainly not a thinking man's Anna Raeburn,
so you must solve your own problems.

Yours sincerely

Jean Rook
Assistant Editor

Enc

Registered in London No 141748.
Registered office: 121 Fleet St London EC4P 4JT

139 Elm Park Mansions
Park Walk
London, S.W.10.

Lord Hugh Scanlon,
The House of Lords,
London, S.W.1.

6th December 1979.

Dear Lord Scanlon,

In spite of your politics, you have always struck me as a plain
man who shoots straight from the shoulder and no monkey-business.
For this reason, I now seek your advice on a matter of some relevance
to myself.

For some time now I have been contributing steadily to both
Tory and Liberal Party funds with, frankly, the intention of being
elevated to the peerage on the recommendation of one or the other.
All is going according to the book and 'discussions' of a confid-
ential nature are now taking place between myself and, on behalf of
the Tories, an agreeable old stick called Major-General Wyldbore-
Smith (I expect you know him) and, on behalf of the Liberals, Miss
Edna McGregor of Flat K8, Sloane Avenue Mansions, London, S.W.3.

However - the recent revelations re moles, pansies and Marxists
in the Establishment have caused me to reconsider my position. I'm
a simple, self-taught man, your Lordship, born, like yourself, below
the salt, and nothing wrong with that, I think you'll agree. A man's
worth is not to be judged by his knowledge of so-called 'art', much
less 'art' of a Neopolitan slant. Here's the nub of it. Have you,
since being raised to the upper house, ever been obliged to mingle
with antique dealers and homosexuals? Is the Establishment rife
with such and is one frequently obliged to take lunch with Rees-Mogg
in Printing House Square with Mr Rubinstein on hand in case of alleg-
ations?

I am prepared to pay a heavy price (financial) to be elevated
to the peerage, but if the price includes eating smoked trout with
Thirties pansies and full Colonels in the KGB I might have to eschew
the honour after all.

Your valuable advise would be esteemed, my Lord, and since you
don't hold yourself out as some sort of Marje Proops of the Upper
House, I enclose a pound to cover your costs in the matter.

Yours sincerely,

Henry Root

Henry Root.

ENGINEERING INDUSTRY TRAINING BOARD

ST MARTINS HOUSE

140 TOTTENHAM COURT ROAD

LONDON   W1P 9LN

01 387 0501

LORD SCANLON
CHAIRMAN

HS/TG   18th December 1979

Henry Root Esq
139 Elm Park Mansions
Park Walk
London SW10

Dear Mr. Root,

　　　　Please forgive the delay in replying to your
letter of 6th December but in addition to being absent
from London, I could not really make up my mind
whether I should reply.   However, I give you my
advice not only freely, but in returning your pound
note, I must emphasize that any official advice would
be much more costly than you can afford.

　　　　If you had been more particular in the choice
of your parents you could now have been in the House
of Lords and one or all of the persons you describe,
and this could not affect your right to take your
seat and all the privileges the House confers.
Because you were not so indulgent, there is nothing
else I can suggest.

                          Yours sincerely,

139 Elm Park Mansions
Park Walk
London, S.W.10.

The Editor,
The Times Educational Supplement,
New Printing House Square,
London, W.C.1.   10th December 1979.

Dear Sir,

My chauffeur has just drawn my attention to an avertisement
for your journal in last week's 'New Statesman' mentioning an
article by someone called Anthony Quinton entitled 'Philosophy
in Small Doses'.

It's clear to me that either you or the aforesaid Quinton
'borrowed' this concept from my own proposed series SEMINAL
THINKERS IN A NUTSHELL Edited by HENRY ROOT, though how my
synopsis happened to fall into your hands I don't entirely
understand. I can only suppose that a mole within Sidgwick and
Jackson Ltd (the only publishing house yet to have seen it) leaked
a copy to you or Mr Quinton.

In case you think I'm testing the wind (as we used to say in
the Navy) I now enclose a copy of my submitted synopsis together
with correspondence applying thereto between myself and Lord
Longford. I think you will agree that the similarity between
'Philosophy in Small Doses' and SEMINAL THINKERS IN A NUTSHELL
Edited by HENRY ROOT is too pronounced to be fortuitous.

I trust this matter can be resolved to my advantage without
recourse to law, Mr Editor, so I look forward to hearing what action
you propose to take to repair some of the damage you have inevit-
ably inflicted on my concept.

I enclose a stamped addressed envelope for the safe return of
my papers after you and your legal advisers have perused them.

Yours faithfully,

Henry Root

Henry Root.

Copy to Michael Rubinstein.

THE TIMES
Higher Education
SUPPLEMENT

Times Newspapers Limited, P.O. Box no. 7, New Printing House Square,
Gray's Inn Road, London WC1X 8EZ (registered office)
Telephone 01-837 1234 Telex 264971 Registered no. 894646 England

From the Editor   December 12, 1979

Dear Mr Root,

Thank you for your letter of December 10.

I can see no possible resemblance between the headline chosen for the article by Mr Quinton and your "seminal thinkers in a nutshell" synopsis.

Yours sincerely,

Peter Scott

Mr Henry Root,
139 Elm Park Mansions,
Park Walk,
London SW 10

139 Elm Park Mansions
Park Walk
London, S.W.10.

Sir Reginald Murley,
The President,
The Royal College of Surgeons,
35 Lincoln's Inn Fields,
London, W.C.2.   15th December 1979.

Dear Sir Reginald,

So - at last someone has had the courage to prescribe publicly
the correct treatment for heartless pickets! Your recent comments
as reported in the papers were an inspiration!

"Debag the cads!" you cried, "and daub them with brightly-
coloured dyes!"

Hear! Hear!

I should like to volunteer as a leading dauber in one of your
debagging squads and to this end I now enclose a pound towards your
initial expenses. These could be heavy, if we're to be as well
organised and quickly on the scene as Sir David McNee's flying
Special Patrol Groups. Might I suggest that, with the exception
of you and me, we recruit for the most-part public schoolboys?
They have most experience of the debagging and application of boot
polish to the water-works of those under them.

I await your instructions, Mr President! I can be ready at
the drop of a scalpel to debag within a radius of fifteen miles
of the above address.

Let's daub the parts of pickets first and ask questions later!

Yours sincerely,

Henry Root

Henry Root.

THE ROYAL COLLEGE OF SURGEONS OF ENGLAND

35-43 LINCOLN'S INN FIELDS, LONDON WC2A 3PN

Telephone 01 405 3474   Cables COLLSURG LONDON WC2

19th December, 1979

OFFICE OF THE PRESIDENT

Sir Reginald Murley, KBE,TD,MSMPRCS.

Dear Mr. Root,

Thank you for your kind letter and the enclosed pound note which I presume is a donation towards supply of gentian violet or other suitable dyes? My letter has evoked an extraordinary number of enthusiastic supporters who have contacted me in various ways. Strangely enough, I have not had any abusive letters nor indeed any reprimands from N.U.P.E. and C.O.H.S.E!

Yours sincerely,

Reginald Murley

President.

H. Root Esq.,
139 Elm Park Mansions,
Park Walk,
London, SW10.

JOHN HUNTER 1728-1793

139 Elm Park Mansions
Park Walk
London, S.W.10.

Lord Hailsham,
The House of Lords,
London, S.W.1.

23rd December 1979.

Dear Lord Hailsham,

I have been much disturbed recently by stories in the press about 'Operation Countryman', the so-called investigation into alleged police corruption in the Metropolitan and City of London forces.

Re-reading that fine man Sir Robert Mark's excellent book 'In The Office of Constable', I came across on page 230 a categorical statement to the effect that he had <u>completely</u> rid the Met of all corruption and wrongdoing (not that there had ever been very much in the first place). With characteristic humility he gives much of the credit for this achievement to those under him. 'Kellend and his men,' he writes, 'and, perhaps, more than anyone else, Jim Starritt, deserve an honoured place in Metropolitan Police history for <u>putting</u> <u>and</u> <u>end</u> <u>to</u> <u>malpractice</u> which had done the force incalculable harm for many year' (italics mine.)

So there we have it in black and white and from the horse's mouth. Since we can assume that Sir Robert is neither ignorant nor dishonest (we have his own word on that), we can conclude that 'Operation Countryman' is a shocking waste of public money and can only have been set up by those engaged on an orchestrated attempt to bring the police into disrepute.

Can you, my Lord, as head of Law and Order inform me why you have not put a stop to this expensive smear campaign?

I should like also to seek your advice on a more purely literary matter. Your opinion seems relevant because I gather you write rhymes and prose yourself and I see from the back of Sir Robert's book that you reviewed it favourably in 'The Sunday Telegraph'. I notice that Sir Robert has frequent recourse to quotation from Shakespeare, not least from Hamlet, the moody Dane.

'I might have been forgiven for thinking with Hamlet,' Sir Robert declaims at one point, 'that "The time is out of joint: 0 cursed spite/That ever I was born to set it right"'

In other parts he uses quotations from the Bard as chapter headings, comparing himself to such as Coriolanus and Mark Anthony (Othello and Bottom the Weaver nowhere get a mention.)

I myself have aspirations as a writer and I would be very grateful if you could inform me as an expert whether frequent references to such as Shakespeare are stylistically desirable, adding ballast to one's manuscript.

Since it is not your function, my Lord, to run a literary or legal advisory service, I enclose a pound to cover the cost of your trouble in these two matters.

Support the Met!

Yours sincerely,

Henry Root

Henry Root.

139 Elm Park Mansions
Park Walk
London, S.W.10.

Mr Robin Day,
'Ask Me Another!',
The BBC,   7th January 1980.
Television Centre,
London, W.12.

Dear Robin,
        I'm prepared to participate as a member of the viewing public
in your popular TV panel show 'Ask Me Another!' If nominated, I
shall put the following question to the team:

        "Do the celebrities think that Mrs Thatcher is the ordinary
man's answer to le vice anglais?"

        In the ensuing discussion I shall play a prominent part, elab-
orating my own thoughts on the matter.

        There'll be some demand to appear on your show, I expect, so,
being a man of the world like yourself, I now enclose a pound to oil
the wheels of my nomination. I enclose too a photo of my head.
As you will see, I am square-built like yourself with a forceful
personality which would show to effect on camera.

        See you in the studio, Robin!

        Yours sincerely,

        Henry Root

        Henry Root.

BRITISH BROADCASTING CORPORATION

LIME GROVE STUDIOS LONDON W12 7RJ

TELEPHONE 01-743 8000 TELEX: 265781

TELEGRAMS AND CABLES: TELECASTS LONDON TELEX

15th January 1980

Mr H Root
139 Elm Park Mansions
Park Walk
London S.W.10

Dear Mr Root

Thank you for your letter to Robin Day of 7th January.

You look a lovely fellow - not, I think, a picture of "head" so much as a portrait of hat and torso! Much as I would like to retain the wheel-oiling green-back, I am unfortunately an employee of the BBC, not a man of the world like yourself!

If you would seriously like to join the audience for "Question Time" one night, I would be only too happy to send you a ticket, or tickets, for the show. I cannot, however, guarantee that you would get a chance to put a question as the subjects debated are chosen on the night from the questions submitted by our audience on arrival - and decided by merit and newsworthiness. However, the opportunity is equal - so if you would like to come please write again or ring me on 01-743-8000 Ext. 3422/3 so we can agree a suitable date.

Thanks again for writing.

Yours sincerely

Barbara Maxwell

Barbara Maxwell
Producer, "Question Time"

Encs.

139 Elm Park Mansions
Park Walk
London, S.W.10.

Miss Barbara Maxwell,
'Question Time',
The BBC,
Lime Grove Studios,
London, W.12.

28th January 1980.

Dear Miss Maxwell,

Thank you for your letter of 15th January in reply to mine of 7th January to Robin Day.

I would indeed be prepared to appear on your excellent quiz show on a date nominated by yourself, and look forward to receiving an entry pass. (One would be sufficient, since I haven't appeared publicly with Mrs Root following a disagreeable incident backstage at the first night of Mr Ray Cooney's spoof musical 'Hullo Dolly').

I look forward to placing many apt questions and trust that Miss Bel Mooney will not be among the celebrities on the panel. I realise that you are now bound by statute to have a token woman on the team, but I suggest that one with rather less to say for herself than Miss Mooney might prove more acceptable. Might it not be a good thing too (with regard to the ratings) to go for a 'looker'? I have in mind such as Miss Fiona Richmond or Miss Vickie Hodge? It's up to you, of course. You know what you're doing.

Please advise me in good time as to my wardrobe.

I look forward to hearing from you.

Yours sincerely,

Henry Root

Henry Root.

139 Elm Park Mansions
Park Walk
London S.W.10.

The Prime Minister,
10 Downing Street,
London, S.W.1

1st January 1980,

Dear Prime Minister,

So - it's honours for big business! Nothing wrong with that!
You were voted into office to promote the interests of your own
class - the lower-middles on their way up - and this is what you're
doing. Well done! The wets and have-nots may bleat, but they have
no one to blame but themselves. They were stupid enough to vote
for you!

How inspiringly your list reads compared to the last one,
which could best have been described as honours for tap dancers
and international criminals! (I gather that 50% of those recognised
were unable to bend the knee at the Palace due to the fact that
they were on Interpol's missing list! No, I'm only chaffing!)

I think the honours that will be greeted with most enthusiasm
by ordinary folk everywhere (apart from those so deservedly con-
ferred on various high street provisioners and drapers) are the
CBE for Norris McWhirter (the runner), the OBE for Emlyn 'The Flying
Pig' Hughes (he can't play for pussy, but he motivates the lads on
and off the ball), the OBE for Cliff Richard for his services to
music (he never did anything discreditable with a chocolate bar)
and the knighthood for John 'What I'm looking for is mediocrity,
laddie!' Junor. I don't normally approve of honours for intellectuals,
but I'm prepared to make an exception in Sir John's case. I'm only
sorry that, if you were going to include thinkers on your list,
you didn't find room for Malcolm Muggeridge, Philip Wrack and
Anna Raeburn. Next year perhaps!

Let's feel the lash of stern government in 1980! Roll back
the nanny state!

Your Man on the Door-Step!

Henry Root

Henry Root.

10 DOWNING STREET

8 January 1980

Dear Mr. Root,

The Prime Minister has asked me to thank
you for your letter of 1 January. She was
grateful to you for writing as you did.
The views which you expressed have been
noted.

Yours sincerely,

J. B. Edmunds

Henry Root Esq

139 Elm Park Mansions
Park Walk
London, S.W.10.

The Editor,
The Daily Express. ('The Voice of Britain'. Well done!)
Fleet Street,
London, E.C.4.
                                    21st January 1980.

Sir,

Like Mrs Patricia M. Edwards, a mother of Westo-super-Mare,
I too read with anger and concern the news in 'The Daily Express'
that Myra Hindley has gained an Open University degree in the
Humanities and is now a BA.

It is an outrage that she should be able to do this while the
unfortunate Mrs Edwards's son has been compelled to discontinue his
own studies due to the retirement of his teacher.

'If my son was in prison,' wrote Mrs Edwards, 'perhaps he
would have that misguided eccentric Lord Longford to compaign for him'.

Precisely! Recently Mrs Root's sister Beryl fell off her
bicycle and broke her pump. This couldn't have happened to Myra
Hindley for the simple reason that bicycles aren't allowed in
Holloway. What has the eccentric Lord Longford got to say to that?

Yours faithfully,

Henry Root.

Henry Root.

c.c.   Lord Longford.

SIDGWICK & JACKSON
Limited
PUBLISHERS

Telegrams: Watergate, London
Telephones: 01-242 6081 2 3

Place of Registration: London, England
Registered Number of Company: 100126

Registered Office:
1 Tavistock Chambers
Bloomsbury Way, London W.C.1A 2SG

7th February 1980

Dear Mr. Root.

Thank you for sending me the letter
that you have written to the Daily Express.

To be quite honest, I wonder if you
are being serious or pulling my leg? You
can't really mean that some one in prison
for fourteen years should be denied educational opportunities, so I assume that you
feel I need a bit of teasing - which may
be true.

Please don't hesitate to telephone
me if you felt that we could make any progress that way.

Yours sincerely,

Longford

Henry Root, Esq
139 Elm Park Mansions
Park Walk
S.W.10

Managing Director: WILLIAM ARMSTRONG
Chairman: THE EARL OF LONGFORD, K.G., P.C.
Joint Deputy Managing Directors: W.D. PROCTER, S. du SAUTOY
Directors: ROCCO FORTE, DAVID KARR (U.S.A.), R.A. SHADBOLT

139 Elm Park Mansions
Park Walk
London, S.W.10.

Lord Hailsham,
The House of Lords,
London, S.W.1.

4th February 1980.

Dear Lord Hailsham,

Congratulations on your recent ruling that, as head of the judiciary, various legal controversies (I refer to the jury rigging debate and the behaviour of judges not least old King-Hamilton) are none of your business. Well done! You've got better things to do than interpose your oar in legal matters.

Not so well done, however, re your failure to reply to my letter of 23rd December 1979 about the shocking waste of public funds involved in so-called 'Operation Countryman'. In the light of Sir Robert Mark's categorical assurance in his excellently written book 'In The Office of Constable' (good title!) that he left the Met as clean as the Aegean stables, I'd aver that 'Operation Countryman constitutes a slander upon Sir Robert's person.

If you have no intention, my Lord, of replying to my points both as to Law and Order and writing style (see my references to Sir Robert's frequent resorting as to Shakespeare and the stylistic desirability thereof) I'd trouble you for my pound back which I appended to my letter of 23rd December.

Thanking you.

Yours sincerely,

Henry Root

Henry Root.

139 Elm Park Mansions
Park Walk
London, S.W.10.

Mr Michael Parkinson,
The BBC,
Television Centre,   14th January 1980.
London, W.12.

Dear Michael,
       I am disappointed not to have heard from you in reply to my
letter of 26th October re 'The Celebrities' Book of Embarrassing
Incidents' and my suggestion that you should co-edit this book
under me.
       Never mind. Such is the viability of the concept that Robson
Books Ltd are keen to proceed with or without your assistance, but
I would still appreciate any 'near-the-knuckle' anecdotes you might
be able to put my way. You must have at your finger-tips a greater
fund of embarrassing (but harmless!) anecdotes than even Niven or
Ustinov.
       So let's hear from you Michael! Remember - it's a fiver an
anecdote and I never met a Yorkshireman who could let pounds sterling
slip down the drain! So get your mind off all that top-drawer
crumpet that I expect comes your way up at the BBC and start recalling
some of the titillating anecdotes you've heard in your time as a
professional celebrity!
       Incidentally, might I congratulate you on your excellent 'chat'
with Miss Twiggy the singing mannequin last week? Many of the 'flat-
chested' cracks were new to me. Well done! And when she spoke of
Fred Astaire the talented old hoofer, your interjection - "They say
he was incapable of a graceless movement!" - was most apt. Are such
off-the-cuff ejaculations scripted or impromptu? You chat show
hosts certainly have to be on your toes!

       I look forward to hearing from you, Michael.
       Yours sincerely,

       Henry Root

       Henry Root.

BRITISH BROADCASTING CORPORATION
TELEVISION CENTRE WOOD LANE LONDON W12 7RJ
TELEPHONE 01-743 8000   TELEX: 265781
TELEGRAMS AND CABLES: TELECASTS LONDON TELEX

4th February, 1980.

Mr. H. Root,
139 Elm Park Mansions,
Park Walk,
LONDON.
SW10

Dear Mr. Root,

My idea is that the kind of book you suggest should
be done for charity and no individual should profit
because the real work in the book is done by the stars
you quote. Therefore, if you are willing to donate
all of your royalties - as I am mine - I might consider
helping, otherwise you are on your own.

Yours sincerely,

Kem O'Mahony

PP

Michael Parkinson

BBC tv

BRITISH BROADCASTING CORPORATION
TELEVISION CENTRE WOOD LANE LONDON W12 7RJ
TELEPHONE 01-743 8000   TELEX: 265781
TELEGRAMS AND CABLES: TELECASTS LONDON TELEX

5th February, 1980.

Mr. Henry Root,
139 Elm Park Mansions,
Park Walk,
LONDON.
SW10

Dear Mr. Root,

I return your £1.

I frankly find your letter offensive.
You can rest assured you will get no
co-operation from either myself or any
member of my team.

Yours sincerely,

Kem O'Mahony

PP · Michael Parkinson

Enc.

139 Elm Park Mansions
Park Walk
London, S.W.10.

Mr John Field,
The News of the World,
30 Bouverie Street,   22nd January 1980.
London, E.C.4.

Dear Mr Field,
        'The Column With The Sunday Punch' has lost nothing since you
took over its authorship from Phillip Wrack. You write crisply and
to the point. Well done!

        I particularly liked your item last Sunday re the crooner Paul
McCartney's arrest in Japan on marijuana charges. Perhaps you could
have pointed out that if this silly young man had landed in Iran he
would have found himself playing the banjo in future with one hand!

        'It is time,' you wrote 'that he learned to live under the same
laws that apply to the rest of us.'

        Hear! Hear!

        Being, like your predecessor and indeed like all the excellent
journalists on your fine newspaper, a stern moralist, you are of the
view, I take it, that we are obliged to obey to the letter even those
laws of which we disapprove. (Leaving aside, of course, the absurd
drink/driving laws which all men of the world ignore). I ask you
this because I find myself clapped in something of a moral paradox.
It seems to me that not only are we obliged to obey all laws (save
the aforementioned), we are also obliged to inform the authorities
when we suspect that a law is being broken. Are you of the opinion,
John, that a citizen failing to do such is aiding and abetting in
the commission of a crime? The fact is that my boy Henry Jr is a
persistent wrong-doer as to the wearing of tights and the smoking of
substances. Despite remonstrances and frequent biffings (spare the
rod etc) he refuses to kick the evil habit in favour of alcohol. Am
I - and here's the crutch of my dilemma - legally obliged to grass
the lad to the local constabulary? And if I don't am I myself breaking the law in that I'm harbouring a wrong-doer? Much as I'd like
to get him into trouble there are those to the left of centre who'd
rule that blowing the whistle on one's own son wasn't cricket. What
would Ritchie Benaud, your cricket correspondent, say?

        I realise that you don't purport to run a drug abuse advice
service, so I enclose a stamped addressed envelope for the courtesy
of your thinking in this matter.

        Yours sincerely,

        Henry Root

        Henry Root. A father.

Mr John Field,
The News of the World,
30 Bouverie Street,
London, E.C.4.

139 Elm Park Mansions
Park Walk
London, S.W.10.

25th February 1980.

Dear Mr Field,

    I am disappointed that you haven't yet replied to my letter
of 22nd January in the matter of Henry Jr's persistent wearing of
tights and smoking of substances, even though I enclosed a stamped
addressed envelope for your convenience. I would point out that
your predecessor as composer of 'The Column With The Sunday Punch!!',
Mr Philip Wrack, always answered my letters with dispatch.

    Never mind. I expect you've been flat to the boards suing
so-called 'Bron' Waugh for his defamatory observations about yourself
and Mr Shrimsley. (I gather he designated the latter 'illiterate'.
How absurd! A careful perusal of the 'News of the World' shows this
to be by no means literally true, so where's Waugh's defence?)

    That said, it must be admitted that suing for libel is a
costly business and since Waugh and 'Private Eye' will no doubt
soon be launching some such childish appeal as 'The Shrimsleyballs
Fund' to defray their expenses, I would like to contribute to your
side of the dispute. Here's a pound, John. Use it to silence
cowardly bullies in the media.

    I look forward to hearing from you re the thrust of my letter
of 22nd January.

    Yours sincerely,

Henry Root

Henry Root.

26 February 1980

Mr H Root
139 Elm Park Mansions
Park Walk
London SW10

Dear Mr Root

Thank you for your letter.   Technically I
suppose it is a citizen's duty to report
law breaking but in practice I am sure that
this will not apply in your case.   Your
problem with your son is very difficult and
really you must make your own decision.
All I can say that in the similar position
I would not go to the police, but instead
I would seek the advise and help of a doctor.

With best wishes.

Yours

John Field

---

28 February 1980

Mr H Root
139 Elm Park Mansions
Park Walk
London SW10

Dear Mr Root

Thank you for your second letter.   I am
sorry about the delay in replying to your
earlier letter which occurred because I
have been involved in another project.
However, I had belatedly replied and this
must have crossed with your second letter.

Mr Shrimsley is very touched by your offer
of £1 towards any possible legal costs.
But he prefers to finance any litigation
with his own funds.   I therefore return
your money with thanks and best wishes.

Yours

John Field

139 Elm Park Mansions
Park Walk
London, S.W.10.

Mr Phil Harris,
PO Equipment Development Division,
93 Ebury Bridge Road,
London, S.W.1.   2nd February 1980.

Dear Mr Harris,

So! Amid the usual orchestrated cries of outrage as the wet left breaks wind and lobbies the so-called NCCL, 'The New Statesman' has blown the whistle on phone-tapping! Big deal! Men of the world such as you and I have known of this sensible practice all along of course. How can you control folk in a free society unless you keep on file their indiscretions?

I should like to take the unusual step of requesting a tap on my own phone (352 9689) unless, that is, I am already on your 'hot target list' as one of the country's top folk of consequence. My reason for making this request is that I'm trying to dump Mrs Root. (She doesn't measure up, you understand, in all respects.) I have been advised by my lawyer Rubinstein that ditching her without good cause might be expensive (I am not without means) and that it is therefore of the essence that I 'get something on her'. It so happens that I have in my possession a letter from a Mr Michael Ivens (head of AIMS, a right-wing pressure group) in which he alleges that Mrs Root was 'known to him' some years ago in the Levant. Alas, all efforts to make this claim stick have proved empty and Rubinstein states that were I to go into court with nothing but this allegement I'd catch a cold.

So there it is. Please tap my phone as from today's date, ignoring my own private calls to such as my 'masseuse', but transcribing all calls between Mrs Root and such of a male tone of voice with whom she may be of a mind to cuckold me, not least the aforesaid Ivens.

I am unsure of the charge for this excellent service, so I enclose a pound on account.

I have marked this letter 'private and confidential' because it occurs to me that, unbeknown to you, your mail may be being 'intercepted' by Mr Brinley Jones of the Post Office Investigation Division. Nothing wrong with that. Quis custodet in corpore sano etc etc.

I await the first transcript.

Yours sincerely,

Henry Root

Henry Root.

Dear Sir

13 February 1980

Reference your letter dated 2 February 1980. I regret that the Post Office cannot supply the information you require and accordingly I return the £1 enclosed with your letter.

Yours faithfully

J. S. J.

Mr H Root
139 Elm Park Mansions
Park Walk
LONDON SW10

139 Elm Park Mansions
Park Walk
London, S.W.10.

Mrs Thatcher,
10 Downing Street,   4th February 1980.
London, S.W.1.

Dear Mrs Thatcher,

In taking retaliatory action against the Soviets re the war
situation post Afghanistan, may I say you have my full support? Of
the various threatened sanctions - the severing of trade agreements,
the cut-back in exchanges at ballet dancer level, the refusal to let
our lads and lassies run and hurdle vis a vis theirs at the Moscow
games and the dispatch of old Lord Carrington on initiatives here
and there (why not swop them Australia for Afghanistan - then they'd
have to cope Kerry Packer?) - the most effective, I think, will be
your intention to drastically step up the broadcasting in their dir-
ection of BBC shows. Several evenings on the trot of seeing nothing
on their screens save mimes awarding one another trophies, 'male'
skaters gaining six out of six for 'artistic impression' and horses
jumping over obstacles at Olympia in the presence of the Queen should
soon have them on their knees pleading for mercy in the matter. Perhaps the sending back to Moscow of Elton John, the bald little warbler
from Weybridge, would put the lid on it.

Mention of horses jumping over things reminds me of a good
Princess Anne joke I heard the other day and which you might care to
utilise in an up-coming speech. (There are those who think your
various pronouncements on this and that sometimes lack for the light
touch and while I appreciate you would normally eschew royal jokes,
I imagine that you'll agree with me that Princess Anne jokes have
become all right since she lost all status by marrying down). Anyway,
here's the joke. At a recent literary luncheon, Miss Jean Rook, the
self-alleged 'Biggest Bitch in Fleet Street', was apprised by her
neighbour of the fact that Princess Anne was looking years younger
these days.

"That's because she's riding older horses," snapped La Rook, as
she likes to be called.

What do you think? Not bad? Use it by all means in a speech,
but perhaps you'd like to credit me along the lines of 'additional
wise-cracks by Henry Root' - something like that.

Here's a pound! Use it to fund the fight against Soviet
adventurism!

Let's dump the doves and rout the wets! (By which I don't
necessarily mean old Willie Wethouse, though he is beginning to wobble
somewhat as to the chops.)

Your man on the doorstep,

Henry Root

Henry Root.

1O DOWNING STREET

30th April 1980

Dear Mr Root,

I am writing on the Prime Minister's behalf
to thank you for your recent letter,
together with the enclosed £1, which I am
returning with this reply.

The contents of your correspondence have
been carefully noted.

With best wishes as always,

Yours sincerely,

Richard Ryder
Political Office

Henry Root Esq

139 Elm Park Mansions
Park Walk
London, S.W.10.

Miss Deirdre McSharry,
'Cosmopolitan',
72 Broadwick Street,
London W1V 2BP.

1st February 1980.

Dear DMcS!,

You won't mind my addressing you as 'DMcS!' since this is how you always end your own lively editorials, a way of signing off which together with the nearby photo of your cheery mug gives your pronouncements a jolly, unpretentious flavour at odds with the 'heavy' feminism of such as Miss Polly Twaddle of 'The Guardian'. Well done! Might I also say, as a mere man, that your magazine is always sharp and caring, dealing in a concerned way with such relevant matters as self-abuse among women and the madness consequent thereon?

Mention of self-abuse and madness brings me to your star 'performer', viable Anna Raeburn. She may be crackers but she's good! It so happens that Robson Books Ltd have recently commissioned me to edit 'The Celebrities' Book of Embarrassing Incidents!' and from the many embarrassing articles contributed by your Miss Raeburn I'd like to quote an extract from her latest emission, which can be taken, I think, as a paradigm of humour. She refers in this article to a recent speaking engagement at a boys' school (lucky lads - as were the lesbians whom Anna recently addressed and who were unable to control themselves! As Anna reported at the time: "They found me a very sexy lady!"), in the course of which the lads asked her as to the differences between her and Jane Lucas, the character in Anna's compassionate documentary 'Agony'. (Incidentally, I wonder if it's occurred to Anna or anyone else to turn this excellent programme into a comedy? Re-written it could be very funny.) In replying, Anna said (and this is the passage I'd like to quote in my upcoming book of celebrities' gags):

'Well, Jane is Jewish. I wish I were but I'm not. Her mother is actually nothing like my mother. Jane drinks coffee - I can't. Actually I think she's a lot nicer than me but she makes the mistake I try not to make. She's on call to the world 24 hours a day. I mean, if my husband had started to make love to me and somebody rang up and told me he was miserable and he had to see me, you wouldn't catch me leaping out of bed, pulling on my clothes and saying "Sorry, honey, got to go, keep - (and I gestured!) warm for me" and rushing for the door!!! Two hundred adolescent boys yelled with mirth and I felt jubilant. Keep the Nobel Prize, the medals, wealth and beauty. I'll settle for being funny every time!"

I'm still chuckling over this, as is Mrs Root, and I'd be most grateful if you'd grant me permission to utilise it in my up-coming humorous book. Thanks DMcS!

One small quibble while I have your ear. At the foot of page 22 it says 'Unfortunately 'Cosmopolitan' cannot accept unsolicited articles and short stories for publication'. I don't get this. If this state of affairs is unfortunate why don't you alter your policy? If, on the other hand, your policy's correct, why do you term it unfortunate? You'd do better to say 'Fortunately Cosmopolitan cannot accept unsolicited articles and short stories for publication.'

All the best DMcS!

Henry Root

Henry Root.

NO REPLY!

139 Elm Park Mansions
Park Walk
London, S.W.10.

Mr Alan Thompson,
The Daily Express,
Fleet Street,
London, E.C.4.

26th February 1980.

Dear Alan,

So they call you 'The Voice of Sport'. Well done!

Since I have plans to enter the writing game myself (though on a rather more serious level than you, I must admit), I wonder whether I could seek your expert advice on a literary matter?

I notice that you often make your comments under the bye-line 'Thommo'. Do you sign yourself thus for the purposes of acquiring a bluff, down-to-earth, man-on-the-terraces image?

Would you advise me to sign my own stuff Rooto? To date I've rendered my work here and there (novels, anthologies, plays etc) as WOMAN WATCHING by HENRY ROOT, SEMINAL THINKERS IN A NUTSHELL edited by HENRY ROOT and THE ENGLISH WAY OF DOING THINGS by HENRY ROOT. Would I have better luck, do you think, were I to submit them as:

WOMAN WATCHING by ROOTO.
SEMINAL THINKERS IN A NUTSHELL edited by ROOTO.
THE ENGLISH WAY OF DOING THINGS by ROOTO.

I'd greatly appreciate your ruling on this point, and I enclose a stamped addressed envelope for the courtesy of your reply.

Yours sincerely,

Henry Root

Henry Root. (Rooto).

DAILY EXPRESS

Express
Newspapers
Limited

121 Fleet Street
London EC4P 4JT
Telephone
01-353 8000
Telex No 21841
Cable Address
Express London

6 March 1980

Mr Henry Root
139 Elm Park Mansions
Park Walk
London
S W 10

Dear Rooto

I am in receipt of your letter and the answer
is yes.

Yours sincerely

Alan Thompson

Registered in London No 141748.
Registered office: 121 Fleet St London EC4P 4JT

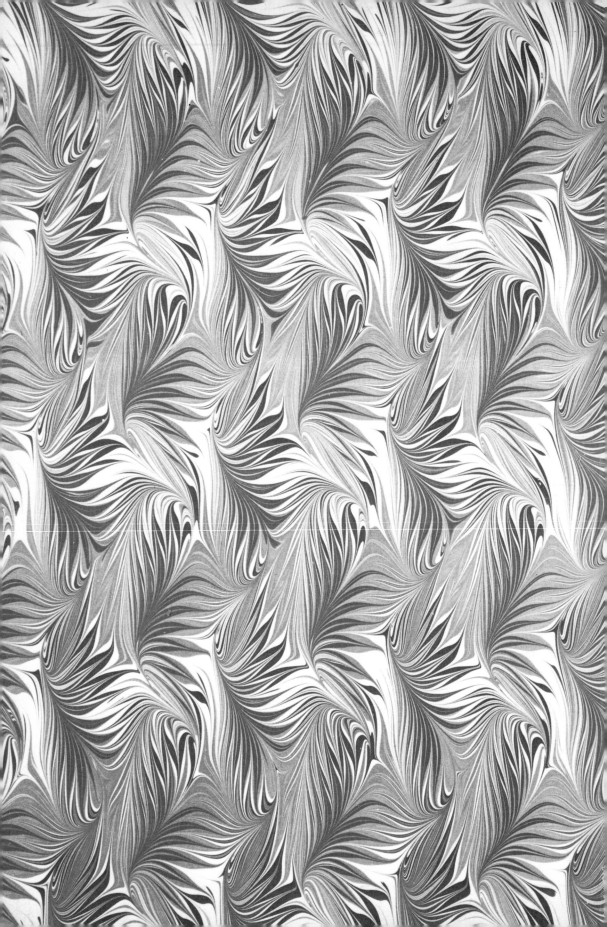